BRITISH SLOW COOKER COOKBOOK

Everyday Recipes for Your Slow Cooker

Copyright©2023 Elijah Griffen

All rights reserved. No part of this book may be reproduced or used in any manner without the prior written permission of the copyright owner, except for the use of brief quotations in a book review.

Printed by Amazon in the USA.

Disclaimer : Although the author and publisher have made every effort to ensure that the information in this book was correct at press time, the author and publisher do not assume and hereby disclaim any liability to any party for any loss, damage, or disruption caused by errors or omissions, whether such errors or omissions result from negligence, accident, or any other cause. this book is not intended as a substitute for the medical advice of physicians.

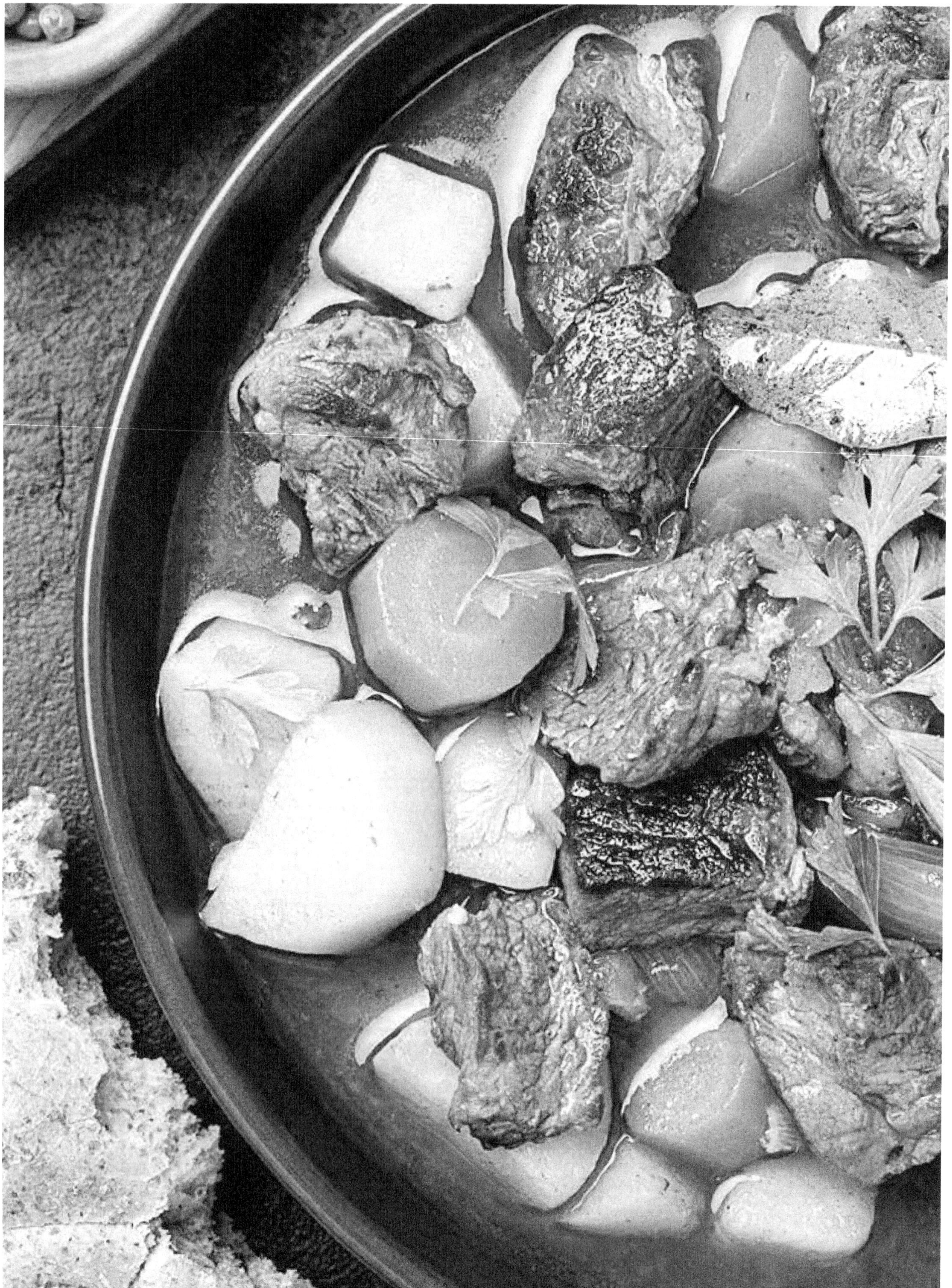

CONTENTS

INTRODUCTION 5

SLOW COOKER RECIPES 9

Slow Cooker Veggie Bolognese.................... 10
Slow Cooker Sticky Sausages With Marmalade....... 11
Slow Cooker Sausage Casserole 12
Easy Slow Cooker Spaghetti Bolognese 13
Slow Cooker Rice Pudding 14
Slow Cooker Summer Vegetable And Butter Bean Stew.. 14
Slow Cooker Butter Chicken........................ 15
Slow Cooker Onion Soup............................. 16
Slow-Cooker Apple-Glazed Ribs 16
Slow Cooker Shepherd'S Pie 17
Slow Cooker Pulled Chicken Tacos 18
Slow Cooker Honey Mustard Chicken 19
Slow Cooker Aloo Gobi................................. 20
Slow Cooker Ratatouille 21
Slow-Cooker Roast Beef 22
Slow Cooker Lamb Shoulder 23
Pot-Roast Turkey Drumstick....................... 24
Slow Cooker Macaroni Cheese 25
Slow Cooker Pork Shoulder With Butterbeans, Apple And Sage 26
Slow Cooker Chickpea Tagine 27
Slow Cooker Massaman Curry.................... 28
Slow Cooker Chicken Curry......................... 29
Slow Cooker Beef Lasagne.......................... 30
Slow Cooker Thai Green Chicken Curry 31

Slow Cooker Vegetarian Hotpot................. 32
Slow Cooker Beef Hotpot 33
Slow Cooker Lamb And Sweet Potato Tagine.......... 34
Slow Cooker Chicken Tikka Masala 35
Slow Cooker Sausage And Lentil Casserole 36
Slow Cooker Barbecue-Style Pork Chops.............. 36
Slow Cooker Aubergine And Cherry Tomato Curry 37
Slow-Cooker Risotto With Fennel, Lemon And Rocket 38
Slow Cooker Chicken Pie Filling 39
Slow Cooker Chicken Pho............................ 40
Slow Cooker Chicken With Lemon And Olives........ 41
Slow Cooker Beef Brisket With Bean Mash 42
Slow Cooker Coq Au Vin............................... 43
Slow Cooker Lamb Shanks.......................... 44
Slow-Cooker Spring Chicken And Herb Soup 45
Slow Cooker Beef Curry............................... 46
Slow Cooker Chicken Casserole With Dumplings ... 47
Slow Cooker Chicken And Vegetable Tagine 48
Easy Slow Cooker Beef Stew....................... 49
Slow Cooker Minestrone 50
Slow Cooker Harissa Vegetable Stew........ 51
Slow Cooker Goulash................................... 52
Slow Cooker Chinese-Style Beef................. 53
Slow Cooker Meatballs In Tomato Sauce................ 54
Slow Cooker Chicken Korma........................ 55

Slow Cooker Lamb Rogan Josh	56
Slow Cooker Dal	57
Slow Cooker Beef Bourguignon	58
Veggie Slow Cooker Curry	59
Slow Cooker Mulligatawny Soup	60
Slow Cooker Honey Roast Ham	61
Slow Cooker Chicken Shawarma	62
Slow Cooker Chicken Noodle Soup	63
Slow Cooker Chipotle Pulled Pork	64
Slow Cooker Chicken Cacciatore	65
Slow Cooker Lentil Soup	65
Slow Cooker Vegan Bean Chilli	66
Slow Cooker Beef Casserole	67
Slow Cooker Chicken Stew	68
Slow Cooker Satay Chicken Wraps	69
Slow Cooker Roast Beef Stew	70
Slow Cooker Chilli Con Carne	71
Slow Cooker Spaghetti Genovese	72
Slow Cooker Bolognese	73
Slow Cooker Black Bean Beef And Rice	74
Slow Cooker Beef Stroganoff	75
Slow Cooker Moussaka	76
Slow Cooker Vegetable Soup	77
Slow Cooker Sesame And Miso Ribs	78
Slow Cooker Roast Chicken	79
Slow Cooker Paprika Chicken	80
Slow Cooker Chicken Soup	81
Slow-Cooked Tomato And Fennel Stew With Pearl Barley	82
Slow Cooker Creamy Chicken, Lemon And Basil Pasta	83
Slow-Cooked Roast Chicken With Gravy	84
Slow Cooker Chocolate Self-Saucing Pudding	85
Veggie Bean Stew	86
Vegetable Casserole With Dumplings	87
Gingerbread With Salted Caramel And Clotted Cream	88
Chipotle Pinto Bean Stew	89
Fennel And Butternut Squash Stew With Cannellini Beans	90
Malva Pudding	91
Mediterranean Bean Stew With Potato Griddle Cakes	92
Red-Red Stew With Spiced Plantain	93
Chickpeas With Harissa And Yoghurt	94
Spicy Autumn Squash Stew	95
Vegan Chilli	96
Aubergine And Black Bean Bowl	97
Ultimate Vegan Stew	98
Greek-Style Beans	99
Black-Eyed Bean Stew	100
Pumpkin Stew With Sour Cream	101
Pulled Jackfruit Coconut Stew	102
Chickpea Stew With Tomatoes And Green Chilli	103
Peanut Stew	104
Flexible Lentil Stew	105
Versatile Vegetable Stew	106
Easy Mexican Bean Stew	107
Cannellini Bean And Pea Stew	108

INTRODUCTION

A slow cooker is an electric countertop cooking appliance that does exactly what it sounds like it does...cooks slowly! It's made up of a large pot with a heating element inside and a ceramic or stainless steel insert. The food is placed into the insert, the pot is covered with a lid, then it's cooked for a long time at a low temperature. The heat starts on the bottom of the insert, then slowly moves up into the food. The lid traps the heat and moisture in the pot and the condensation that forms on the underside of the lid falls back onto the food as it cooks. This keeps the food super moist even as it cooks for a long length of time.

WHAT IS THE POINT OF A SLOW COOKER?

- Ease: Many slow cooker recipes are dump and go. No fancy layers or fuss, just dump the ingredients and continue on with your busy day.

- One-Pot Meals: Many slow cooker recipes are one-pot meals. This means no need for side dishes, and no need for extra dishes. All the cleanup you have is the slow cooker insert.

- Keeps Food Warm: Planned for dinner at 5 and didn't get home until 6? No problem. The slow cooker keeps food warm and ready for when you are.

- Great for Tough Meats: Slow cooking is the best way to break down tougher cuts of meat so they're fall-apart tender in texture, and retain their moisture in the process. No babysitting required.

- Develop Deep Flavor: Soups and stews that have longer cooking times develop great flavors.

CAN YOU SEAR IN A SLOW COOKER?

Most slow cookers, no. A traditional slow cooker does exactly what it says...cooks slowly. Searing means you are cooking something quickly at high heat. Some slow cookers now offer that function, but not all. Be sure to read the functions of the product. In certain recipes, you may be instructed to sear meats before adding them to the slow cooker. This helps them get that crispy exterior that the slow cooker can't achieve.

CAN YOU COOK GROUND BEEF IN A SLOW COOKER?

Totally! You can put raw ground beef into the slow cooker and it cooks perfectly. You can use ground beef in a specific recipe or you can cook it on its own to add to another recipe. The main thing you need to know is that cooking anything in the slow cooker does require a liquid. So even cooking plain ground beef will require the addition of water or broth. This prevents the beef from drying out or burning on the bottom of the insert. Also, keep in mind that by cooking the ground beef in the slow cooker directly, you will not be able to drain any excess fat.

Slow cookers are a classic kitchen appliance that, when understood properly, can make home-cooking so much easier. They're great for cooking in bulk and for prepping ahead of time. You can enjoy meats, soups, stews, pastas, dips, and even desserts! Slow cookers allow you to set it and forget it, and even cook from frozen! Yes – a slow cooker is the tool to give any beginner cook, as well as a trusty sidekick to any seasoned chef.

WHAT'S THE DIFFERENCE BETWEEN A SLOW COOKER AND A CROCKPOT?

There isn't one! Technically, there is no appliance called a "crockpot". CrockPot is the brand that developed the first slow cooker. Now, even though there are other brands that make slow cookers, the terms "slow cooker" and "crockpot" are still used interchangeably to refer to the same appliance.

SLOW COOKER RECIPES

Slow Cooker Veggie Bolognese

A really rich vegetarian slow cooker bolognese that's perfect for serving with spaghetti or made into a veggie lasagne, pasta bake or cottage pie. It makes six generous servings, keeps well in the fridge for a couple of days and can be frozen for 4 months.

Servings: 6 **Cooking Time: 2 Hours**

Ingredients:

- 2 tbsp sunflower, vegetable or light olive oil
- 1 medium onion, finely chopped
- 2 garlic cloves, crushed
- 2–3 medium carrots, about 200g/7oz, peeled and cut into small chunks
- 200g/7oz mushrooms, any kind, sliced
- 2 x 400g tins green lentils, drained and rinsed
- 400g tin chopped tomatoes
- 150ml/5fl oz hot vegetable stock, made with 1 stock cube
- 3 tbsp tomato purée
- 2 tsp caster sugar
- 1 tsp dried oregano
- 2 dried bay leaves, or 1 fresh
- salt and freshly ground black pepper
- freshly cooked pasta, grated cheese and basil, to serve (optional)

Directions:

1. Heat the oil in a large non-stick frying pan and fry the onion over a medium–high heat for about 3 minutes or until lightly browned, stirring regularly. Add the garlic and cook for 1 minute more.
2. Tip the onion and garlic into the slow cooker and add the carrots, mushrooms, lentils, tomatoes, stock, tomato purée, sugar and herbs. Season with salt and lots of freshly ground black pepper. Cover the slow cooker with its lid and cook on high for 4–5 hours or low for 6–8 hours.
3. Serve with freshly cooked pasta, grated cheese and fresh basil, if you like.

Notes:

1. You can use any mushrooms you like for this bolognese, but small chestnut mushrooms work particularly well. Slice your mushrooms (not too thinly), or quarter them if they're small.
2. You can use 1 tsp garlic granules or powder instead of fresh garlic in this recipe if you like.
3. You can use any tinned lentils for this bolognese. Sachets of lentils work too (although they are more expensive), or add tinned beans or chickpeas instead if you have some handy.

Slow Cooker Sticky Sausages With Marmalade

With just six ingredients, this mustard and marmalade sausage casserole is sure to become a weeknight go-to. Browning the sausages first is more about appearance than flavour, so feel free to skip that bit if you don't mind what the finished bangers look like.

Servings: 4   Cooking Time: 2 Hours

Ingredients:

- 150g/5½oz marmalade
- 85g/3oz wholegrain mustard
- 200g/7oz dried cannellini beans, soaked and boiled (400g prepped weight, see Tip)
- 2 red onions, cut into wedges
- 550g/1lb 4oz carrots, peeled and cut into long, chunky batons
- 8 pork sausages
- salt and freshly ground black pepper

Directions:

1. Place the sausages in a non-stick frying pan (or in a normal frying pan with a splash of vegetable oil) over a high heat and fry until browned all over.
2. Mix the marmalade and mustard with 500ml/18fl oz water until combined. Add the ingredients to the slow cooker in even layers: the partly cooked cannellini beans, then the onions, then carrots and finally sausages. Pour the mustardy-marmalade sauce all over (don't mix). Season with salt and pepper, cover with the lid and turn the slow cooker to low.
3. Cook for 6 hours, stirring after about 4 hours if you're home, until the beans and carrots are tender. For a stickier finish, balance the lid so the pot is partly uncovered and turn the slow cooker to high for the final 30 minutes of the cooking time.
4. Season with salt and pepper and stir before serving.

Notes:

1. Any leftovers can be frozen for up to 2 months.
2. We've used dried cannellini beans as they're better value than tinned. However, some beans contain a protein called lectin, which can cause illness if not cooked at high temperatures. For safety, we've soaked the beans (at least 5 hours is good but overnight is ideal) and boiled them in a pan of water for 10 minutes before slow cooking. You can do this in large batches and freeze what you don't need right away.
3. If you've already boiled your beans, you'll need 400g of them (prepped weight) for this recipe.
4. Alternatively, if your budget allows, use 1½ tins of cannellini beans and you can skip the soaking and boiling.

Slow Cooker Sausage Casserole

Browning the sausages and onion at the beginning doesn't take long and will add lots of extra flavour to this simple slow cooker casserole. Serve with some green veg if you like – broccoli, cabbage, green beans or frozen peas work well.

Servings: 4   Cooking Time: 2 Hours

Ingredients:

- 2 tbsp vegetable or sunflower oil
- 1 medium onion, thinly sliced
- 12 chipolata sausages
- 3–4 medium carrots, around 300g/10½oz, peeled and cut into 2cm/¾in slices
- 600g/1lb 5oz medium floury potatoes, preferably Maris Piper, peeled and cut into 3–4cm/1½in chunks
- 400g tin chopped tomatoes
- 200ml/7fl oz hot chicken or vegetable stock, made with 1 stock cube
- 3 tbsp tomato purée
- 1 tsp dried mixed herbs
- salt and freshly ground black pepper

Directions:

1. Heat 1 tablespoon of the oil in a large non-stick frying pan and fry the onion over a high heat for 3–4 minutes, until lightly browned, stirring often. Tip into the slow cooker.
2. Add the remaining oil to the frying pan and fry the sausages over a medium-high heat for 4-5 minutes, or until browned on all sides.
3. While the sausages are frying, add the carrots, potatoes and chopped tomatoes to the slow cooker.
4. Mix the hot stock with the tomato purée and herbs. Pour into the slow cooker and season with salt and pepper; stir well. Place the sausages on the tomato and vegetable mixture without stirring in – this will help them retain their colour and texture.
5. Cover the slow cooker with its lid and cook on high for 5–6 hours, or low for 7–9 hours.

Notes:

1. Chipolata sausages work well here, as they can be easily divided and served, but you can also use a larger sausage without affecting the cooking time at all.
2. It's best to choose a floury variety of potato for this recipe, so a Maris Piper or King Edward is ideal. They will soften more quickly than a waxy variety. Serve with care so they don't break up too much.
3. Try and pick a tin of good quality tomatoes for the best flavour, or if using a value tin add 1 tsp caster sugar to give the sauce some extra sweetness.

Easy Slow Cooker Spaghetti Bolognese

Try this family-style bolognese sauce in your slow cooker – it makes four very generous servings or easily stretches to six when served with lots of spaghetti. It keeps well in the fridge for a couple of days and freezes brilliantly for up to four months.

Servings: 6　　　**Cooking Time: 2 Hours**

Ingredients:

- 500g/1lb 2oz beef mince
- 1 medium onion, finely chopped
- 2 garlic cloves, crushed
- 200g/7oz mushrooms, any kind, sliced
- 400g tin chopped tomatoes
- 275ml/9½fl oz hot beef stock, made with 1 beef stock cube
- 3 tbsp tomato purée
- 1 tsp dried oregano
- 2 dried bay leaves, or 1 fresh
- salt and freshly ground black pepper
- freshly cooked spaghetti, grated cheese and basil, to serve

Directions:

1. Put the mince and onion in a large non-stick frying pan and fry together over a medium–high heat for about 4 minutes, stirring and squishing against the side of the pan with a couple of wooden spoons to break up the mince as much as possible.
2. Add the garlic and cook for 1 minute more.
3. Tip the mince and onions into the slow cooker and add the mushrooms, tomatoes, stock, tomato purée and herbs. Season with salt and lots of freshly ground black pepper.
4. Cover the slow cooker with its lid and cook on high for 4–5 hours or low for 6–8 hours.
5. When ready, serve the Bolognese sauce with freshly cooked spaghetti, some grated cheese and basil, if you like.

Notes:

1. You can use any mushrooms you like for this Bolognese, but small chestnut mushrooms work particularly well. Slice your mushrooms (not too thinly), or quarter them if they're small.
2. You can use 1 tsp garlic granules or powder instead of fresh garlic in this recipe, if you like. If using a value can of tomatoes, add 1 tsp of sugar to the pot to balance the flavour.
3. If you have any leftover red wine knocking about, use 100ml/3½fl oz and reduce the stock by the same amount, so the total liquid quantities stay the same.

Slow Cooker Rice Pudding

If you prefer your rice pudding cold, make it with 900ml/1½ pint of milk instead, and the rice pudding will continue to thicken as it cools. Top with a dollop of any flavour jam.

Servings: 4   Cooking Time: 2 Hours

Ingredients:

- 15g/½oz butter
- 100g/3½oz pudding rice
- 750ml/1¼ pint full-fat milk
- 25g/1oz caster sugar, ideally golden caster sugar
- ¼ tsp ground or grated nutmeg (optional)
- 4 heaped tbsp jam, to serve

Directions:

1. Grease the inside of your slow cooker pot generously with the butter. Put the rice, milk and sugar in the dish. Add a little nutmeg if you like.
2. Stir gently, then cover with the lid and cook on low for 3–4 hours, or until the rice is tender and creamy. Divide between four dishes and top with jam.

Slow Cooker Summer Vegetable And Butter Bean Stew

An easy-going, vegan, slow-cooked summer veg stew. Serve as a main course with crusty bread to mop up the juices, or as a warm salad along with other sharing plates.

Servings: 2-3   Cooking Time: 2 Hours

Ingredients:

- 2 red, orange or yellow peppers, roughly diced
- 1 small courgette, diced
- ½ aubergine, diced
- 1 small red onion, finely sliced
- 1 small fennel bulb (or ½ a large one), finely sliced
- 3 large ripe tomatoes, finely diced
- 2 large garlic cloves, crushed
- small handful fresh oregano leaves, roughly chopped, or ½ tsp dried oregano
- 15g/½oz basil, plus extra small leaves to serve
- 3 tbsp extra virgin olive oil, plus extra to serve
- 60g/2¼oz marinated olives in oil
- 400g tin butter beans, drained
- 1 tbsp sherry vinegar or balsamic vinegar
- salt and freshly ground black pepper
- fresh bread, to serve

Directions:

1. Preheat the slow cooker to high.
2. Add all the chopped veg to the slow cooker pot and stir in the garlic, oregano, half the basil and the olive oil. Season generously with salt and pepper, cover with the lid and cook for 2 hours.
3. Stir in the olives, butter beans and vinegar and cook for another 15–20 minutes until the veg is all tender. Taste and adjust the seasoning. Stir through the remaining basil.
4. Finish with a scattering of small basil leaves and a drizzle of olive oil. Serve with plenty of fresh bread.

Slow Cooker Butter Chicken

Use your slow cooker to make a rich, creamy butter chicken curry that's perfect for all the family. Serve with rice or naan bread to soak up all the lovely sauce.

Servings: 4   Cooking Time: 2 Hours

Ingredients:

- 20g/¾oz butter, cut into small chunks
- 4 garlic cloves, not too large, finely grated
- 20g/¾oz chunk fresh root ginger, peeled and finely grated
- 4 tsp medium curry powder
- ¼ tsp dried chilli flakes
- 2 tbsp tomato purée
- 1 tbsp caster sugar
- 8 boneless, skinless chicken thighs, each cut into 4 similar sized pieces
- 100ml/3½fl oz double cream
- salt and freshly ground black pepper
- basmati rice and fresh coriander, to serve

Directions:

1. Put the butter, garlic, ginger, curry powder, chilli flakes, tomato purée and sugar in the slow cooker and combine thoroughly.
2. Add the chicken, season well with salt and pepper and mix with the spice mixture until coated on all sides. Add 75ml/2½fl oz cold water and stir well.
3. Cover the slow cooker with its lid and cook on high for 4–5 hours until the chicken is very tender and the sauce smells sweet and aromatic.
4. Pour the cream into the slow cooker, cover and cook on high for a further 10 minutes, or until hot. Adjust the seasoning to taste and serve with freshly cooked rice and fresh coriander.

Notes:

1. This curry is best cooked fairly quickly, but you can switch to low and cook for 5–6 hours if that suits your timings better.
2. If you like a spicier curry, increase the curry powder by 1 tsp and add an extra ½ tsp dried chilli flakes.
3. The sauce for this chicken isn't overly thick and the final results will depend a little on the size of your slow cooker and how long you cook the chicken. If you like more sauce, simply add extra cream at the end, or drizzle a little over when you serve.

Slow Cooker Onion Soup

This is a super-easy and happily budget-friendly soup with just five ingredients. The slow cooker does all the work here, caramelising and intensifying the flavours of the onion for a rich-tasting result.

Servings: 4   Cooking Time: 2 Hours

Ingredients:

- 30g/1oz butter, diced
- 800g/1lb 12oz onions, thinly sliced
- 1½ tsp roughly chopped thyme leaves (optional)
- 1½ tsp sugar
- 1.2 litres/2 pints beef or vegetable stock (made from 2 beef or vegetable stock cubes)

Directions:

1. Toss the butter, onions, thyme (if using) and sugar together in the bowl of the slow cooker. Put the lid on and cook on high for 6–8 hours, stirring every so often, until the onions are rich and caramelised.
2. Pour in the stock and cook for another 30 minutes. Serve hot.

Slow-Cooker Apple-Glazed Ribs

Think you can't make ribs on a weekday? Pop them in the slow-cooker and you can have meltingly tender ribs any day. Crisp up on the barbecue for extra deliciousness.

Servings: 4   Cooking Time: 2 Hours

Ingredients:

- 75ml/2¾fl oz ready-made apple sauce
- 2 tbsp honey
- 1 tsp Worcestershire sauce
- 1 tsp smoked paprika
- 1 tsp Chinese five-spice powder
- 1kg/2lb 4oz pork ribs, cut into individual ribs
- salt and freshly ground black pepper

Directions:

1. Mix the apple sauce, honey, Worcestershire sauce and spices together in a large bowl until well combined.
2. Season the ribs well with salt and freshly ground black pepper, then add them to the bowl and mix well to completely coat them in the apple glaze.
3. Transfer the ribs to the slow cooker and cook on a low heat for 7-8 hours, or until the meat is falling off the bone.
4. To serve, divide the apple-glazed ribs among 4 serving plates and serve with sweetcorn, spicy baked beans and mashed potatoes.

Slow Cooker Shepherd'S Pie

Make your shepherd's pie mix in the slow cooker for ease, then top with creamy mashed potato and finish in the oven. This recipe freezes beautifully, so divide into smaller portions if you like. Serve what you need and freeze the rest for up to 3 months.

Servings: 6   **Cooking Time: 2 Hours**

Ingredients:

- 500g/1lb 2oz lamb mince
- 1 medium onion, finely chopped
- 1 celery stick, trimmed and thinly sliced (optional)
- 1 tbsp plain flour
- 275ml/9½fl oz hot lamb stock, made with 1 stock cube
- 3 tbsp tomato purée
- 3 tbsp Worcestershire sauce
- 3–4 medium carrots, about 300g/10½oz, peeled and cut into 1.5cm/½in chunks
- 1 tsp dried mixed herbs
- salt and freshly ground black pepper
- For the potato topping
- 1.2kg/2Ib 10oz potatoes, ideally Maris Piper, peeled and cut into 3–4cm/1½in chunks
- 75g/2 2/3oz butter, cubed
- 100ml/3½fl oz milk

Directions:

1. Put the mince, onion and celery in a large non-stick frying pan and fry together over a medium–high heat for about 5 minutes, stirring and squishing against the side of the pan with a couple of wooden spoons to break up the mince as much as possible.
2. Tip the mince, onion and celery into the slow cooker and toss with the flour. Mix the hot stock with the tomato purée and Worcestershire sauce and pour over the mince. Add the carrots and herbs. Season with salt and lots of freshly ground black pepper and stir well.
3. Cover the slow cooker with its lid and cook on high for 4½–5½ hours or low for 7–9 hours. (Cover and cook for a further 10 minutes if not baking afterwards.)
4. Preheat the oven to 220C/200C Fan/Gas 7. Twenty minutes before the mince is ready, simmer the potatoes in a large pan of water for about 15 minutes or until soft. Drain well, then return to the pan and add the butter along with plenty of salt and pepper. Mash together. Add the milk and mash until smooth. (Warm the milk first if not baking in the oven afterwards.)
5. Transfer the mince mixture to a shallow ovenproof dish and top with the mashed potatoes, using a large metal spoon and starting at the outside of the dish and working your way through to the centre. Bake for 25–30 minutes or until the top is lightly browned. Serve alongside your choice of vegetables.

Notes:

1. Use your own favourite recipe for the mash if you prefer, or simply serve the mince with mash or boiled potatoes on the side.
2. Add 50g/1¾oz finely grated cheese to the mashed potatoes if you like and sprinkle a little extra over the topping just before baking.
3. If saving leftovers, reheat the shepherd's pie from frozen for the best results.

Slow Cooker Pulled Chicken Tacos

This slow cooker pulled chicken recipe is perfect piled into tacos and wraps, or used as a filling for jacket potatoes. It uses affordable, easy-to-find ingredients the whole family will love. If you like a little more heat, add ½-1tsp dried chilli flakes or chilli powder to the pot.

Servings: 4-6　　Cooking Time: 2 Hours

Ingredients:

- 100g/3½oz tomato ketchup
- 4 tbsp runny honey
- 3 tbsp Worcestershire sauce
- 75ml/2½fl oz orange juice (see tip)
- 1 tsp hot smoked paprika
- 2 garlic cloves, thinly sliced, or 1 tsp garlic granules
- 6–8 boneless, skinless chicken thighs
- salt and freshly ground black pepper
- To serve
- mini flour tortillas, warmed
- soured cream
- fresh coriander, chopped
- limes, cut into wedges

Directions:

1. Put the ketchup, honey, Worcestershire sauce, orange juice, paprika and garlic in the slow cooker. Sprinkle with a generous pinch of salt and plenty of freshly ground black pepper and mix well.
2. Add the chicken thighs and turn to coat in the sauce. Move the thighs away from the sides of the pot so they don't stick when the sauce reduces as it simmers.
3. Cover and cook on low for 5–7 hours, or until the chicken is very tender.
4. Remove the lid and use two forks to break up and shred the chicken while mixing with the sweet, smoked sauce. The sauce will thicken the longer the chicken is cooked, so ladle a little out before shredding the chicken if cooking for the shorter time.
5. To serve, spoon the chicken into warmed mini tortillas along with soured cream and fresh coriander. Serve with lime wedges for squeezing.

Notes:

1. If you are short on time, switch your slow cooker to high and the chicken will be ready in about 3 hours. The sauce will still be fairly liquid at this point, but you can transfer to a saucepan and simmer on the hob for a 4–5 minutes until reduced, before pouring back over the chicken.
2. Use orange juice from a carton or the freshly squeezed juice of 1 orange should give around 75ml/2½fl oz.

Slow Cooker Honey Mustard Chicken

Golden chicken thighs in a creamy mustard and honey sauce makes a great family supper, especially as you prepare it in a slow cooker. It might seem like a lot of mustard but the flavour softens during cooking, leaving just a hint that complements the sweetness of the honey perfectly. Serve with green veg and potatoes or rice.

Servings: 4   Cooking Time: 2 Hours

Ingredients:

- 1 tsp sunflower, vegetable or light olive oil
- 6–8 chicken thighs, with skin and bone-in
- 300ml/10fl oz hot chicken stock, made with 1 stock cube
- 2 tbsp mustard, English, wholegrain or a combination
- 2 tbsp runny honey
- ½ tsp dried mixed herbs
- 4 tbsp double cream
- 1 tbsp cornflour mixed with 1 tbsp cold water
- salt and freshly ground black pepper

Directions:

1. Heat the oil in a large non-stick frying pan over a medium-high heat. Season the chicken thighs on all sides with salt and freshly ground black pepper. Fry the chicken thighs, skin-side down, for 3–5 minutes or until crisp and golden. Turn and cook on the other side for 2 minutes. Frying the chicken will give it a lovely colour and render out some of the fat that sits just below the skin, but take care as it can spit a little as it fries.
2. While the chicken is frying, pour the stock into the slow cooker and stir in the mustard, honey and herbs until thoroughly mixed. Add the chicken pieces to the slow cooker, skin-side up, cover and cook on high for 3–4 hours.
3. Once the chicken is cooked, gently stir in the cream and cornflour mixture, cover and cook for a further 10 minutes or until the sauce thickens. (If your chicken releases lots of fat into the pot, you may want to spoon a little off before adding the cream.)
4. Serve the chicken hot with the sauce and lots of freshly cooked vegetables, with potatoes or rice on the side.

Notes:

1. This slow cooker recipe cooks best on high for a shorter time but you can also cook on low for 4–6 hours if that suits your timings better, switching to high when you add the cream and cornflour.
2. Pack sizes of chicken thighs vary, but you should aim for one large chicken thigh, or quarter, or two smaller thighs per person. If you end up with an uneven number, don't worry too much, the chicken is so tender that it can be pulled off the bone and divided very easily.
3. Any mustard works for this recipe, but I like to use 1 tbsp each of English mustard and wholegrain mustard if I have both handy.

Slow Cooker Aloo Gobi

A great veggie curry that's mild enough to suit all tastes. If you like it spicier, cook with a whole green chilli, pricked a couple of times with a fork. Just make sure to fish it out before serving!

Servings: 4   Cooking Time: 2 Hours

Ingredients:

- 2 tsp cumin seeds
- 2 tsp nigella seeds (optional)
- 4 large garlic cloves, crushed
- 1 tbsp grated fresh root ginger (or ginger purée)
- 500g/1lb 2oz tomatoes, chopped (or 400g tin chopped tomatoes)
- 4 tsp mild curry powder
- 2 tsp turmeric
- 3 tbsp butter or ghee
- 1 tbsp tomato purée
- 500g/1lb 2oz new potatoes, larger ones halved or quartered
- 1 cauliflower, head chopped into small florets and leaves saved (see Tips below)
- salt and freshly ground black pepper
- To serve
- freshly cooked rice or warmed naan bread
- plain yoghurt

Directions:

1. Turn the slow cooker to the High setting to heat up. Toast the cumin and nigella seeds, if using, in a small frying pan for 1 minute until fragrant. Tip into the slow cooker with the rest of the ingredients and ½ teaspoon salt.
2. Cook for 3 hours on Low, until the potatoes are tender. Season well with salt and pepper and serve with rice or naan bread, yoghurt and cauliflower leaves (see Tips), if desired.

Notes:

1. Shred up the cauliflower leaves. Heat 1 tablespoon vegetable oil or ghee in a frying pan and fry the shredded leaves over a high heat with 1 teaspoon nigella seeds, a pinch of sugar and some salt and pepper. When starting to brown but still crunchy, squeeze in some lemon juice, stir fry for 1 minute more and serve with the aloo gobi or any curry.

Slow Cooker Ratatouille

Tender Mediterranean vegetables in a rich tomato and garlic sauce are a cinch to prepare in a slow cooker. Ratatouille will keep well in the fridge for up to three days.

Don't be tempted to skip some of the olive oil here as it adds a real silkiness to the sauce. Serve just warm or at room temperature with fresh basil and lots of crusty bread or as an accompaniment to grilled meats and fish – it even works as a pasta sauce.

Servings: 6   Cooking Time: 2 Hours

Ingredients:

- 6 tbsp extra virgin olive oil
- 1 medium aubergine, cut into roughly 3cm/1¼in chunks
- 2 medium red onions, thinly sliced
- 4 garlic cloves, very thinly sliced
- 2 medium courgettes, halved lengthways and cut into roughly 2cm/¾in slices
- 1 large red pepper, cut into roughly 3cm/1¼in chunks
- 1 large yellow pepper, cut into roughly 3cm/1¼in chunks
- 400g tin chopped tomatoes
- 2 tbsp tomato purée
- 2 tsp caster sugar
- 1 tsp dried oregano
- 2 dried bay leaves, or 1 fresh bay leaf
- salt and freshly ground black pepper

Directions:

1. Heat 2 tbsp of the oil in a large non-stick frying pan and fry the aubergine for 3–5 minutes over a high heat, or until lightly browned on all sides. Tip onto a plate and return the pan to the heat.
2. Add another 2 tbsp of the oil and fry the onions for 3 minutes or until lightly browned, stirring constantly. Add the sliced garlic over and fry together for a few seconds more.
3. Tip the onions and garlic into the slow cooker and add the courgettes, peppers, tomatoes, tomato purée, oregano, sugar and bay leaves. Drizzle with the remaining oil and season with salt and lots of freshly ground black pepper. Stir well.
4. Scatter the aubergine pieces on top of the vegetables, but don't stir in. Cover the slow cooker with its lid and cook on high for 3½–4½ hours, or low for 5½–7 ½ hours. Stir lightly and adjust seasoning to taste before serving.

Notes:

1. Scattering the aubergine on top without stirring in will help it retain its shape.

Slow-Cooker Roast Beef

This all-in-one slow cooker roast beef joint means you don't have to lose your weekend in the kitchen to enjoy a traditional Sunday roast dinner. The beef is meltingly tender and stays juicy. It's not one for those who like a rare roast, but rather more for pot roast fans.

Servings: 6 **Cooking Time: 2 Hours**

Ingredients:

- 1–2 tbsp olive oil
- 1.2kg/2lb 12oz beef brisket joint
- 2 onions, halved
- 1.4kg/3lb 3oz medium–large, similarly sized, floury potatoes, such as Maris Piper
- 6 carrots, peeled and trimmed
- 4 tbsp cornflour
- 1 tbsp dried mixed herbs or herbes de provence
- 1 tsp English mustard powder
- 1 tbsp tomato purée
- 1 tbsp Worcestershire sauce
- 1 tbsp yeast extract
- 200ml/7fl oz red wine (optional, see recipe tip)
- 1 beef stock pot
- 1 litre/1¾ pint boiling water
- salt and freshly ground black pepper
- 900g/2lb mixed green vegetables, cooked, to serve

Directions:

1. Preheat the slow cooker to the lowest setting.
2. Place a large, heavy-based frying pan over a high heat. Rub the oil all over the brisket joint, then season well with salt and pepper. Sear in the pan on all sides until well coloured all over. Lift into the slow cooker.
3. Push the onion halves into the gaps around the beef, then the potatoes, and finally fit the carrots over and around the top. Put the kettle on.
4. Put half of the cornflour, the mixed herbs and mustard powder in a measuring jug. Use a fork to mash in the tomato purée, followed by the Worcestershire sauce and yeast extract. Gradually pour in the red wine until you have a smooth paste and all the wine is incorporated.
5. Add the beef stock pot then the boiling water. Pour this mixture all over the beef and vegetables, put the slow cooker lid on and cook for 9 hours. The beef and vegetables should be meltingly tender.
6. Carefully lift the beef, carrots and potatoes onto a platter and cover with foil to keep warm. Pour everything else into a wide saucepan and bring to the boil.
7. Mash a small amount of the gravy into the remaining cornflour to make a smooth paste. Whisk back into the rest of the gravy.
8. Boil until reduced by about a third and thickened to a gravy. At this stage you can discard the onions – or if you love slow-cooked onions, slice and mix with the other vegetables.
9. Pull apart the beef into large chunks using a pair of forks. Discard any leftover fat. Push the beef to one side of the platter and arrange the vegetables alongside – halving the potatoes as you go.
10. Season the gravy with salt and pepper, spoon a little over the beef and vegetables, then put the rest into a jug and serve with plenty of green veg and the sides of your choice.

Notes:

1. Cooking a joint of beef in the slow cooker isn't hard, but the result can depend on the beef joint you choose. Brisket is a great value cut of beef – perfect for long, gentle cooking in a slow cooker. But silverside and topside

work well too.

2. If you can get 6 medium–large potatoes that each weigh about 225g/8oz – perfect!
3. If you don't want to use the red wine, just add the equivalent amount more beef stock.

Slow Cooker Lamb Shoulder

For dinner, slowly cooking this lamb shoulder on low is ideal, but for lunch cook on high to save yourself an early start.

Servings: 5-6   Cooking Time: 2 Hours

Ingredients:

- 3 garlic cloves, crushed or finely chopped
- 2 rosemary sprigs, needles picked and finely chopped (or 2 tsp dried)
- 2 tsp olive oil
- 1 lamb shoulder (about 1.5kg/3lb 5oz), boned and rolled
- 1 large onion with skin left on, thickly sliced
- 2 small carrots, trimmed, scrubbed and halved lengthways
- 600ml/20fl oz hot lamb stock (made with a stock pot if possible)
- 2 tbsp redcurrant jelly, plus extra to serve
- 2–4 tbsp cornflour (or gravy granules, see tip)
- salt and freshly ground black pepper
- fresh rosemary or thyme sprigs, to garnish (optional)
- mint sauce, to serve

Directions:

1. Mix the garlic, rosemary, oil, 1 teaspoon salt and some black pepper together in a small bowl. Rub all over the lamb.
2. Place the onion and carrot in the base of a slow cooker in an even layer, then sit the joint of lamb on top. (If you're preparing ahead, put the slow cooker pot in the fridge and chill overnight.) Pour in the stock, add the redcurrant jelly and cover with the lid. Cook on high for 5–5½ hours or low for 8–9 hours, flipping the joint over halfway through, until the lamb is really tender.
3. If you'd like to crisp up the lamb skin, preheat the grill to high and place the lamb in a roasting tin. Remove any string then grill until the top of the joint is golden brown – it will only take a few minutes.
4. To make the gravy, strain the liquid from the slow cooker into a saucepan. Spoon off most of the fat that rises to the top (or use a fat separator).
5. Mix 1 tablespoon of the liquid into 2 tablespoons cornflour in a small bowl, then whisk back into the rest of the liquid. Simmer over a medium heat until thickened, then season to taste with salt and pepper. If the gravy is still too thin for your liking, repeat with the remaining cornflour.
6. Garnish the lamb with the rosemary, if preferred, then serve with the gravy, more redcurrant jelly and mint sauce.

Notes:

1. If you'd like to intensify the flavour of the gravy, substitute 1–2 tbsp cornflour with lamb or beef gravy granules. Add in the same way, simmering on the hob until thickened.
2. The size of the lamb joint you can cook depends on the size and shape of your slow cooker. Make sure you don't buy one that's too big.

Pot-Roast Turkey Drumstick

Turkey is not just for Christmas! The drumsticks cost very little and stretch a long way - perfect for a meaty pot-roast on a modest budget.
This pot-roast can be cooked in advance and frozen, check the tips section for freezing instructions.

Servings: 3-4   Cooking Time: 2 Hours

Ingredients:

- 1 x 825g/1lb 13oz turkey drumstick
- 2 tbsp sunflower oil
- 4 carrots, trimmed
- 4 celery sticks, trimmed
- 1 onion, roughly chopped
- 1 tsp dried mixed herbs
- 1 bay leaf
- 1 chicken stock cube
- 500ml/18fl oz just-boiled water
- 150ml/5fl oz red wine (or chicken stock)
- 2 tbsp tomato purée
- 2 tbsp redcurrant jelly or cranberry sauce
- 300g/10½oz small new potatoes, scrubbed and halved
- 1 tbsp cornflour
- salt and freshly ground black pepper

Directions:

1. Preheat the oven to 170C/150C Fan/Gas 3. Season the turkey drumstick all over with salt and pepper.
2. Heat the oil in a flameproof, lidded casserole over a medium heat. Add the turkey drumstick and fry for 4-5 minutes, turning regularly until lightly browned on all sides. Transfer to a plate and set aside.
3. Chop the carrots and celery into roughly 2.5cm/1in lengths. Add the onion, celery and carrot to the casserole and fry for 4-5 minutes, stirring regularly. Stir in the herbs and bay leaf and continue to cook for a further 30-40 seconds.
4. Dissolve the chicken stock cube in the just-boiled water, then pour it into the casserole along with the wine (or extra chicken stock). Stir in the tomato purée and the redcurrant jelly (or cranberry sauce) and return the turkey drumstick to the mixture.
5. Cover the casserole with the lid and transfer to the oven. Cook for 1½ hours. After 1½ hours, add the new potatoes to the casserole, turn the turkey drumstick over, then replace the lid and continue to cook for a further 1½ hours, or until the turkey is very tender and the meat is falling off the bone.
6. Remove the turkey drumstick from the casserole and transfer it to a chopping board. Set aside until cool enough to handle. Meanwhile, spoon as much fat as possible from the surface of the casserole.
7. In a small bowl, whisk the cornflour with a tablespoon of cold water to form a thick paste. Stir this paste into the pot-roast sauce. Heat the sauce until it is simmering and continue to stir until thickened.
8. While the sauce is thickening, remove the skin from the turkey drumstick, then remove the meat from the bone in large chunks, discarding any bone or sinew.
9. To serve, spoon the pot-roast sauce into bowls and place equal amounts of the turkey meat on top of each portion. Serve with freshly steamed green cabbage.

Notes:

1. Tip 1: Follow the method up to the point that the turkey and vegetables go into the oven, using just 250ml/9fl oz just-boiled water to make the stock, and transfer all the ingredients to a large slow cooker. Cover and cook on high for 5 hours, turning the drumstick and adding the potatoes after 2½ hours. Remove the turkey leg, spoon

of the excess fat then add the cornflour mixture to the pot, cover and cook for 5 minutes or until thickened, stirring.
2. Tip 2: If making this dish in advance, freeze the turkey meat, off the bone, with the sauce and vegetables (but without the potatoes) in a freezer-proof container for up to 3 months. Thaw overnight in the fridge then reheat in a suitable dish in the microwave until piping hot throughout, stirring at least once.

Slow Cooker Macaroni Cheese

This is a fab no-hassle way to make macaroni cheese. You may find the timings vary a bit between slow cookers. The most important thing is not to let the pasta overcook and turn to mush.
Each serving provides 608 kcal, 29g protein, 62g carbohydrates (of which 10g sugars), 26g fat (of which 16g saturates), 4g fibre and 1.2g salt.

Servings: 6   Cooking Time: 2 Hours

Ingredients:

- 400g/14oz dried macaroni
- 200g/7oz extra mature cheddar, coarsely grated
- 200g/7oz ready-grated mozzarella, from a packet
- 410g can evaporated milk
- freshly ground black pepper

Directions:

1. Put the macaroni and both types of cheese in a slow cooker.
2. Pour over the evaporated milk and add 700ml/1¼ pint of water. Season with pepper and stir.
3. Cover and cook on high for 1½ hours, or until all the cheese has melted and the pasta is almost tender. Stir really well, then cover and cook for a further 15 minutes, or until the pasta is tender but holding its shape.
4. Serve immediately – the longer the pasta sits, the softer it will become.

Notes:

1. It's important to use ready-grated mozzarella for this recipe for a consistently smooth sauce.
2. If you like, you can transfer to a flame-proof dish, sprinkle with more grated cheese and grill until golden

Slow Cooker Pork Shoulder With Butterbeans, Apple And Sage

Crispy fried sage adds a special touch to this easy slow-cooker pork recipe.

Servings: 4   Cooking Time: 2 Hours

Ingredients:

- 2 onions, roughly chopped
- 2 sticks celery, thinly sliced
- small bunch fresh sage
- salt and freshly ground black pepper
- 2 x 400g/14oz cans butterbeans in water, rinsed and drained
- 4 thick pork shoulder steaks
- 1 tbsp olive oil
- 400ml/14fl oz dry cider
- 100ml/3½fl oz strong, good quality chicken stock
- 30g/1oz butter
- 1 Braeburn apple, peeled
- 1 tsp cornflour mixed with 1 tbsp cold water until smooth
- 1 tbsp wholegrain mustard

Directions:

1. Place the onions, celery and five shredded sage leaves in a slow cooker, then season with salt and freshly ground black pepper. Scatter with the butterbeans.
2. Season the pork steaks with salt and freshly ground black pepper. Heat the oil in a non-stick frying pan then fry the pork until golden-brown on both sides. Transfer to the slow cooker.
3. Pour the cider and stock into the frying pan, then bring to the boil. Pour over the pork, put the lid on, then cook on low for seven hours until tender and surrounded with sauce.
4. Cut the apple into eight wedges and cut away the core. Heat the butter in a frying pan, then add the butter and fry for 8-10 minutes until golden-brown and just tender. Add about 15 more sage leaves, turn up the heat and fry until the leaves are crisp.
5. Lift the pork steaks from the slow cooker and set aside in a serving dish. Mix the cornflour paste and the mustard into the beans and stir till the sauce thickens a little. Transfer the sauce to the serving dish with the pork, top with the apples and crisp fried sage. Serve with crusty bread and a crisp green salad.

Slow Cooker Chickpea Tagine

This healthy and comforting tagine is packed with flavour and delicious served over simple couscous or crisp baked potatoes.

Each serving provides 310kcal, 6g protein, 46g carbohydrate (of which 31g sugars), 9g fat (of which 1.5g saturates), 9g fibre and 0.7g salt.

Servings: 4   Cooking Time: 2 Hours

Ingredients:

- 400g/14oz can chickpeas in water, rinsed and drained
- 1 red pepper, deseeded and thickly sliced
- 1 onion, chopped
- 1 small butternut squash, peeled, deseeded and cut into bite-sized pieces
- 2 courgettes, cut into bite-sized pieces
- 12 dried apricots
- salt and freshly ground black pepper
- 2 tbsp extra virgin olive oil, plus a drizzle to serve
- 2 garlic cloves, crushed
- 2 tsp paprika
- 1 tsp ground ginger
- 1 tsp ground cumin
- 500g/1lb 2oz carton passata
- 2 tsp honey, plus a drizzle to serve
- 1 tsp harissa paste
- handful fresh mint or coriander
- thick Greek-style yoghurt, to serve

Directions:

1. Place the chickpeas, pepper, onion, squash, courgettes and apricots into a slow cooker and season with salt and freshly ground black pepper. Heat the oil in a frying pan, then fry the garlic and spices until fragrant, about one minute. Add the passata, honey and harissa, then bring to a boil.
2. Pour the sauce over the vegetables, cover with the lid and cook on high for four hours.
3. Season to taste with plenty of salt and freshly ground black pepper. Tear in most of the mint or coriander leaves, stir through, then scatter the remaining leaves over the top. Drizzle with a little more oil and honey, then top with spoonfuls of yoghurt. Serve with couscous.

Slow Cooker Massaman Curry

A fragrant and filling southern Thai dish with peanuts and potatoes - a delicious slow cooker alternative to Thai green curry.

Servings: 4　　Cooking Time: 2 Hours

Ingredients:

- 500g/1lb 2oz new potatoes, halved
- 800g/1lb 12oz boned lamb shoulder or beef shin, cut into matchbox-size pieces
- 3 tbsp massaman curry paste
- small bunch fresh coriander, stalks finely chopped
- 5cm/2in piece fresh root ginger, finely grated
- 400ml/14fl oz can coconut milk
- 1 tsp light muscovado sugar
- 1 lime, zest and juice
- 1 tbsp fish sauce, plus extra to taste
- 6 freeze-dried makrut lime leaves (optional)
- handful roasted unsalted peanuts, roughly chopped, to serve

Directions:

1. Place the potatoes in the slow cooker. Heat a large non-stick frying pan and brown the meat in batches until golden brown, then transferring to the slow cooker. There's no need to add any oil to the pan as the meat is fatty enough.
2. Add the massaman paste, coriander stalks and ginger to the frying pan, then fry for a few minutes until fragrant.
3. Tip in the coconut milk and bring to the boil. Season with the sugar, lime zest and fish sauce, add the lime leaves if using, then pour the sauce over the meat and potatoes. Cover with the lid and cook on low for 8 hours until very tender.
4. Spoon off any excess fat from the top of the curry, add the juice from half the zested lime and add more fish sauce if needed. The curry should have a balance of sour, salty, hot and sweet without one flavour dominating. Scatter with the coriander leaves and peanuts, then serve with steamed fragrant rice and the remaining lime in wedges, for squeezing.

Notes:

1. Take care as you stir the curry, as the meat will be very tender and can easily break up.

Slow Cooker Chicken Curry

This Maylasian-style, coconutty, veg-packed slow cooker chicken curry is easy to prepare for the family. It's mild enoug for all the family.
Equipment and preparation: For this recipe, you will need a 4.5 litre/8 pint slow-cooker.

Servings: 4-5   Cooking Time: 2 Hours

Ingredients:

- For the curry paste
- 2 onions, quartered
- 20g/¾oz fresh root ginger, peeled, coarsely grated
- 6 garlic cloves, peeled
- 2 tbsp medium curry powder
- 1 tsp dried chilli flakes
- 1 tsp ground turmeric
- 2 tbsp sunflower oil
- For the curry
- 8 chicken thighs, boned, skinned, halved
- 1 cinnamon stick
- 3 star anise
- 500g/1lb 2oz large waxy potatoes, peeled, cut into 3cm/1¼in chunks
- 3 carrots, peeled, sliced into 1.5cm/½in rounds
- 2 tbsp cornflour
- 400ml tin coconut milk
- 150g/5oz green beans, trimmed and cut in half
- freshly ground black pepper

Directions:

1. Put all of the curry paste ingredients in a food processor and blend. You will need to remove the lid and push the mixture down a couple of times using a rubber spatula.
2. Heat a large, non-stick frying pan over a medium heat. Spoon in the curry paste and cook for 2-3 minutes, stirring constantly, until fragrant.
3. Season the chicken thighs on all sides with lots of pepper.
4. Add the chicken thighs, cinnamon and star anise to the pan, stir well and cook for 2-3 minutes, turning the chicken pieces once or twice until they are pale golden-brown.
5. Stir in 100ml/3½fl oz water and bring the mixture to the boil. Transfer to the slow cooker and add the potatoes and carrots.
6. In a bowl, whisk 2 tablespoons water with the cornflour to form a thin paste. Stir in the coconut milk and pour over the curry. Stir well to combine.
7. Cover and cook on high for 3 hours, or until the chicken and vegetables are tender and the sauce has thickened. Just before the end of the cooking time, stir in the green beans.
8. Serve the curry just as it is, or with small portions of steamed rice.

Notes:

1. Tip 1: If preferred, substitute the green beans with a sliced pepper.
2. Tip 2: It's important to use waxy potatoes because floury potatoes will fall apart during the long cooking time.

Slow Cooker Beef Lasagne

With layers of rich meaty tomato sauce, tender pasta and luscious cheese sauce this easy slow cooker beef lasagne will fast become a family favourite.

Servings: 4   Cooking Time: 2 Hours

Ingredients:

- For the meat sauce
- 4 tbsp olive oil
- 500g/1lb 2oz beef mince
- 1 medium red onion, finely chopped
- 2 garlic cloves, finely chopped
- 2 sticks celery, finely chopped
- 1 medium carrot, peeled and finely chopped
- 1 tbsp dried mixed herbs
- 400g tin chopped tomatoes
- salt and freshly ground black pepper

- For the white sauce
- 125g/4½oz mascarpone
- 250g/9oz ricotta
- 50ml/2fl oz whole milk
- 150g/5½oz strong cheddar, grated
- To assemble and garnish
- 9 dried lasagne sheets
- 10g/1/3 oz fresh basil leaves, roughly torn, to garnish (optional)

Directions:

1. To make the meat sauce, heat 2 tablespoons of olive oil in a large frying pan over a medium-high heat. Add the mince and season with salt and pepper, then fry for 10 minutes, breaking up the mince with a wooden spoon as it cooks, until browned all over. Remove the mince from the pan and set aside.
2. Return the pan to a medium heat and add the remaining 2 tablespoon of oil along with the chopped onion, garlic, celery and carrot. Season again with salt and pepper, then cook for about 10 minutes, stirring often, until the vegetables are slightly softened and look glossy.
3. Return the mince to the pan and add the dried herbs and tinned tomatoes. Fill the empty tin one-quarter full with cold water, swill around and tip into the pan.
4. Bring everything to a simmer, check the seasoning and add a little more salt and pepper if needed, then turn off the heat.
5. To make the white sauce, whisk together the mascarpone, ricotta, milk and 100g/3½oz of the cheddar in a bowl.
6. To assemble the lasagne, pour one-third of the white sauce into the bottom of your slow cooker, top with 3 lasagne sheets, breaking up as necessary to cover the meat. Spoon over one-third of the meat sauce.
7. Repeat the layers with the remaining sauces and pasta sheets, finishing with the meat sauce. Sprinkle the top with the remaining cheddar.
8. Cook on high for 3 hours or low for 5 hours. By the end of cooking the pasta sheets should be tender and the centre of the lasagne piping hot.
9. Just before serving, garnish with the fresh basil, if using.

Notes:

1. Do not be tempted to remove the lid during the cooking as this will allow heat to escape and increase cooking time.
2. Swapping the layers of sauce around so the meat sauce is uppermost (rather than the usual white sauce) means

you get a golden top which is hard to achieve in a slow cooker. If you prefer you can assemble the lasagne in the traditional way and use a chef's blow torch to brown the top after cooking.

3. If you have time, it helps the lasagne to firm up and keep its shape if you can let it sit for a while before removing it from the slow cooker dish (or make it a day ahead and chill in the fridge overnight). Don't worry if you can't – it's delicious either way.

Slow Cooker Thai Green Chicken Curry

Bulking out a curry with vegetables is a great way to stretch a small amount of meat to keep the cost down. But, if preferred, simply swap the sweet potatoes and edamame beans for two extra chicken thighs.

Servings: 4   Cooking Time: 2 Hours

Ingredients:

- 6 chicken thighs, skin removed and boneless, cut into 4–5cm/1½–2in chunks
- 6 tsp Thai green curry paste
- 400ml tin coconut milk, light or full-fat
- 2 tsp brown sugar, plus extra to serve (optional)
- 2 tsp fish sauce, plus extra to serve (optional)
- 300g/10½oz sweet potatoes (about 1 large one), peeled and cut into 2cm/¾in chunks
- 100g/3½oz frozen edamame beans
- 5 spring onions, trimmed and cut into 3–4cm/1¼–1½in chunks
- 2 tsp cornflour (optional)
- salt and freshly ground black pepper
- 2 limes, 1 juice only and 1 cut into wedges
- freshly cooked sticky or jasmine rice, to serve

Directions:

1. Turn the slow cooker to the High setting to heat up. Add the chicken pieces and stir in the Thai green curry paste. Add the coconut milk, sugar and fish sauce with 100ml/3½fl oz water. Cook the curry on High for 2 hours or Low for 5 hours.
2. Stir in the sweet potato. Cook for 1 hour on High until the potato is soft and the chicken is really tender. Stir in the edamame beans and spring onions and cook for another 10–15 minutes.
3. If you would like the curry sauce to be a little thicker, mix a splash of the sauce with the cornflour in a frying pan to create a smooth paste. Gradually stir in another ladleful of sauce and cook over a medium heat, stirring until the sauce thickens dramatically. Stir this mixture back into the curry in the slow cooker.
4. When the curry is ready, taste and add some of the lime juice and more fish sauce and sugar, if using. Season with salt and pepper, taste and add more lime juice, fish sauce, sugar or seasoning if needed. Serve the curry with the rice and the lime wedges alongside.

Notes:

1. The vegetables in this recipe can be swapped with whatever is in the fridge. Peppers, butternut squash, broccoli and baby sweetcorn can be added when there is an hour left of cooking time and leafier things like pak choi, spinach and frozen peas can be added when there is 15 minutes left of cooking time.

Slow Cooker Vegetarian Hotpot

This slow-cooker vegetarian stew with fluffy dumplings is a cheap and easy recipe. To make it vegan, use vegetable suet in the dumplings instead of butter and omit the pesto. This dish is perfect for batch cooking, just divide it up into indiviudal portions and you will always have warming stew at your fingertips, check the tips section for freezing instructions.

Equipment and preparation: For this recipe you will need a 6.5 litre/11½ pint slow cooker. This meal provides 629 kcal, 13g protein, 79g carbohydrate (of which 24g sugars), 29g fat (of which 11g saturates), 16g fibre and 1.8g salt per portion.

Servings: 4   Cooking Time: 2 Hours

Ingredients:

- For the hotpot
- 2 tbsp sunflower oil
- 1 small butternut squash (approximately 800g/1lb 12oz), scrubbed, deseeded and chopped into chunks
- 2 onions, thinly sliced
- 3 carrots, peeled and cut into chunks
- 2 parsnips, peeled and cut into chunks
- 2 tbsp plain flour
- 400g tin chopped tomatoes
- 2 tbsp tomato purée
- ½ tsp dried chilli flakes (optional)
- 3 tbsp pesto (optional)
- 350ml/12fl oz hot vegetable stock (made with 1 stock cube)
- 100g/3½oz young spinach leaves (optional)
- salt and freshly ground black pepper
- For the dumplings
- 200g/7oz self-raising flour
- 75g/2¾oz frozen butter (or 75g/2¾oz shredded vegetarian suet)
- 125ml/4fl oz cold water
- salt and freshly ground black pepper

Directions:

1. Heat the oil in a large, non-stick frying pan over a medium heat. Add the vegetables, in batches if necessary, and fry for 4–5 minutes, stirring regularly, until lightly browned all over. Season with salt and pepper.
2. Transfer the vegetables to the slow cooker, sprinkle over the flour and stir well. Add the chopped tomatoes, tomato purée, chilli flakes and pesto, if using, and stir again. Pour over the stock and stir. Cover and cook on high for 4 hours.
3. After the hotpot has been cooking for 3½ hours, make the dumplings. Put the flour in a large mixing bowl and season with salt and pepper.
4. Coarsely grate one-quarter of the frozen butter into the flour. Toss the mixture to coat the butter lightly in the flour. Add the remaining butter in three more batches, grating and tossing it in the same way. This should prevent the dumpling dough from clumping and yield light, fluffy dumplings.
5. Stir in enough cold water to bring the mixture together as a soft, squidy dough. Divide into 12 equally sized pieces and roll each into a ball.
6. Remove the lid from the slow cooker, stir in the spinach until wilted, then arrange the dumplings gently on top. Replace the lid and continue to cook on high for a further 25–30 minutes, or until the dumplings are puffed up and fluffy.
7. Spoon the hotpot onto serving plates with the dumplings on top.

Notes:

1. Tip 1: The butternut squash keeps its shape better during cooking if it is left unpeeled. The skin is edible, but you can remove it when eating the hotpot if preferred.
2. Tip 2: A tablespoon of dried mixed herbs can be added to the dumpling dough if desired.
3. Tip 3: To freeze the stew, portion it into separate containers, it will last in the freezer for up to 2 months.
4. Tip 4: To freeze the dumplings, put them on a tray, making sure there is space between them. Put the tray in the freezer, once the dumplings are solid you can divide them into freezer bags.

Slow Cooker Beef Hotpot

Packed with flavour and meltingly tender beef, try this classic comfort food with steamed rice and greens. Each serving provides 212kcal, 20g protein, 14g carbohydrate (of which sugars 13g), 8g fat (of which 2.5g saturates), 2g fibre and 2.8g salt.

Servings: 6   Cooking Time: 2 Hours

Ingredients:

- 1 onion, chopped
- 2 carrots, cut into 1cm/½in slices
- 1 tbsp vegetable or sunflower oil
- 500g/1lb 2oz beef brisket, trimmed of excess fat and cut into matchbox-size cubes, or long, thick slices
- 5 garlic cloves, crushed or finely chopped
- 5cm/2in piece fresh root ginger, finely grated
- 1 fat red chilli, shredded (I leave the seeds in)
- 2 tbsp light muscovado sugar
- 1 tbsp miso paste, optional, but this will add extra depth to the sauce
- 6 tbsp light soy sauce
- 300ml/½ pint beef stock
- 1 tsp sesame oil, plus more to serve
- 2 bunches spring onions, trimmed then cut into finger-length pieces
- few handfuls fresh beansprouts

Directions:

1. Place the onion and carrots into a slow cooker. Heat the oil in a large non-stick frying pan, then fry the beef in two batches until golden-brown, transferring to the slow cooker when ready. Scatter with the garlic, ginger and chilli.
2. Stir the sugar, miso, soy, stock and sesame oil into the juices in the frying pan then bring to a simmer, stirring to dissolve the miso and sugar. Pour the hot liquid over the beef and vegetables, cover with the lid and cook on low for 7½ hours.
3. Scatter with the spring onions, re-cover the slow cooker then cook for another 30 minutes until the onions are tender. Stir in the beansprouts, then drizzle with a little more sesame oil. Serve with steamed broccoli abd boiled rice.

Slow Cooker Lamb And Sweet Potato Tagine

Lamb tagine is a classic and this slow cooker recipe uses the best of Moroccan ingredients. Each serving provides 532 kcal, 33g protein, 65g carbohydrates (of which 21g sugars), 13g fat (of which 4.5g saturates), 12g fibre and 2g salt.

Servings: 6   Cooking Time: 2 Hours

Ingredients:

- For the tagine
- 600g/1lb 5oz lamb neck fillet, trimmed of any excess fat and cut into 3cm chunks
- 2 tbsp harissa paste
- 3 garlic cloves, finely chopped or grated
- 1 tsp ground cumin
- 1 tsp ground coriander
- 1 tsp ground cinnamon
- 1 tsp smoked paprika
- 1 onion, roughly chopped
- 90g/3¼oz dried apricots, roughly chopped
- 90g/3¼oz drained pitted green olives
- 1 x 400g tin chopped tomatoes
- 1 x 400g tin chickpeas, drained and rinsed
- 500g/1lb 2oz sweet potatoes, peeled and cut into chunks
- 350ml/12fl oz chicken stock, from a cube
- 90g/3¼oz low-fat plain yoghurt
- 1 small bunch coriander, roughly chopped
- ½ tsp sea salt
- freshly ground black pepper
- For the couscous
- 200g/7oz couscous
- 1 lemon, zest and juice
- 1 tsp ground cumin
- 1 tsp sweet smoked paprika
- 1 red onion, finely chopped
- 2 green peppers, deseeded and roughly chopped
- ½ chicken stock cube
- 250g/9oz cherry tomatoes, halved, quartered if large
- 1 small bunch mint, leaves picked and roughly chopped

Directions:

1. Preheat the slow cooker on the high setting.
2. Put the lamb into the slow cooker. Add the harissa paste, garlic, spices, salt and pepper and mix well. Add the onions and apricots, olives, chopped tomatoes, chickpeas, sweet potato and chicken stock. Stir well and cover with the lid.
3. Leave the tagine to cook on high for 6–8 hours, or on low for 8–10 hours.
4. Put the couscous into a large bowl, add the lemon zest and juice, ground cumin, smoked paprika, onion and peppers and stir well. Add the chicken stock cube and pour over 250ml/9fl oz boiling water. Cover with cling film and leave for 10 minutes.
5. Use a fork to fluff up the couscous, then stir through the cherry tomatoes and mint.
6. Serve the tagine with the couscous, top with a dollop of yoghurt and finish with a scatter of chopped coriander.

Slow Cooker Chicken Tikka Masala

One of the UK's favourite curries, chicken tikka masala is traditionally made in three stages. Firstly, the chicken is marinated in spiced yoghurt, then chargrilled to give it a delicious lick of smoke and finally simmered in a spicy tomato sauce. This simple recipe makes it easy to create at home in a slow cooker for tender results.

Servings: 4   Cooking Time: 2 Hours

Ingredients:

- For the marinade
- 8 chicken thighs, boneless and skinless, cut into bite-sized pieces
- 1½ tsp fine sea salt
- ½ lemon, zest and juice
- 200g/7oz full-fat natural yoghurt
- 2 garlic cloves, finely grated
- 20g/¾oz fresh root ginger, peeled and finely grated
- 1 tbsp garam masala
- 1 tsp smoked paprika
- 1 tsp turmeric
- 1 tsp ground cumin
- pinch chilli powder
- For the grilled onions
- 2 medium onions, cut into small cubes (approx. 1cm/½in)
- 2 tbsp olive oil
- 1 tsp smoked paprika
- 1 tsp turmeric
- pinch chilli powder
- 1 tbsp garam masala
- For the sauce
- 2 tbsp butter
- 1 tbsp tomato purée
- 400g tin chopped tomatoes
- 50ml/2fl oz double or whipping cream
- salt and freshly ground black pepper
- To serve
- 10g/1/3 oz fresh coriander

Directions:

1. Place the chicken pieces in a large bowl and add the salt, lemon zest and juice and mix well. Add the remaining marinade ingredients and stir to combine. Cover and chill in the fridge for at least 3 hours or overnight.
2. When ready to cook the chicken, line a grill tray with foil and heat the grill to high.
3. Place the chicken in a single layer on one side of the grill tray, transferring any excess marinade back into the bowl. Spoon this remaining marinade into your slow cooker.
4. To prepare the grilled onions, toss together the onions, oil, smoked paprika, turmeric, chilli powder and garam masala in a bowl. Season well with salt and pepper, then lay the onions on the other side of the grill tray.
5. Grill the chicken and onions for around 12 minutes, turning the chicken and moving the onions halfway through cooking. This stage is to add colour to the chicken, rather than fully cook it.
6. Add the chicken and onions, together with any juices from the grill tray, to the slow cooker along with the sauce ingredients of butter, tomato purée and tinned tomatoes. Stir well and lightly season with salt and pepper.
7. Cook for 2 hours on high or 4 hours on low.
8. When ready to serve, check the seasoning and adjust with a little more salt and pepper if needed. Stir through the cream and sprinkle with coriander to finish.

Slow Cooker Sausage And Lentil Casserole

Fennel and pork are a lovely combination in this slow cooker sausage and lentil stew. Healthy lentils add extra fibre and protein. You don't need anything with this, but, if you do fancy something on the side, try some crusty bread to mop up the sauce.

Servings: 4   Cooking Time: 2 Hours

Ingredients:

- spray oil
- 375g/13oz pork chipolata sausages (about 12 sausages)
- 1 bulb fennel, finely sliced, leafy fronds reserved for garnish
- 200g/7oz dried green lentils
- 700ml/1¼ pint chicken stock
- 2 bay leaves (optional)
- large pinch fennel seeds, ground
- 2 small onions, thinly sliced
- 1 fat garlic clove, crushed
- 125ml/4fl oz dry white wine

Directions:

1. If necessary, preheat your slow cooker. Heat a little spray oil in a frying pan set over a high heat. Once hot, add the sausages and fry until browned all over.
2. Meanwhile, add the fennel, lentils, chicken stock, bay leaves (if using) and fennel seeds to the slow cooker.
3. Transfer the browned sausages to the slow cooker. Using the same pan, gently fry the onions until softened. Add the garlic and fry for a minute. Turn up the heat and add the wine, let it bubble for a minute, then tip the contents of the pan into the slow cooker. Season generously with salt and pepper and give it a stir.
4. Cover with a lid and cook on high for 4 hours, or low for 7–8 hours. Serve in warmed bowls garnished with the reserved fennel fronds.

Slow Cooker Barbecue-Style Pork Chops

Add five ingredients that you're likely to have in the store cupboard to pork chops, and simply give the slow cooker 8–10 hours to do the hard work in this simple supper.

Servings: 4   Cooking Time: 2 Hours

Ingredients:

- 400g/14oz can chopped tomatoes
- 4 tbsp clear honey
- 2 tbsp tomato ketchup
- 2 tbsp dark soy sauce
- ½ tsp hot smoked paprika
- 4 thick pork chops (each about 170g/6oz)
- ground black pepper
- boiled rice, to serve
- cooked corn on the cob, to serve (optional)

Directions:

1. Mix the tomatoes, honey, ketchup, soy sauce and smoked paprika thoroughly in a slow cooker. Season with ground black pepper.
2. Add the pork and turn to coat in the sauce. Cover and cook on low for 8–10 hours, or until the sauce is thick and glossy and the pork is tender. Serve with cooked rice and corn on the cob, if you like.

Slow Cooker Aubergine And Cherry Tomato Curry

This veggie-packed aubergine and cherry tomato curry uses rogan josh paste to make a light and healthy summer lunch or supper. There is a little on-the-hob prep to be done here, but it really helps to bring out the flavours before it all goes into the slow cooker.

Servings: 4   Cooking Time: 1-2 Hours

Ingredients:

- 2 tbsp olive oil
- 1 large onion, finely sliced
- 2.5cm/1in piece fresh root ginger, peeled and grated
- 3 large garlic cloves, finely chopped
- 70g/2½oz rogan josh curry paste
- 1 large aubergine, diced
- 1 cinnamon stick
- 400g/14oz cherry tomatoes
- 100g/3½oz Greek yoghurt
- small bunch fresh coriander, chopped, plus extra to serve
- a squeeze of lemon juice, plus lemon wedges to serve
- salt
- cooked rice, to serve

Directions:

1. Preheat the slow cooker to high.
2. Meanwhile, heat the oil in a large frying pan over a medium heat, add the onion and cook for about 8 minutes until golden.
3. Add the ginger, garlic and curry paste and cook for a few more minutes. Add the aubergine and stir well to coat it with the spices, then tip everything into the slow cooker and add the cinnamon stick. Cook for 45 minutes.
4. Stir in the cherry tomatoes and cook for another 45 minutes, until the aubergine is tender and the tomatoes are bursting.
5. Gently stir in the yoghurt and coriander, being careful not to break up the tomatoes too much. The sauce should be thick and creamy; add a dash of water if you feel it's too thick.
6. Add the coriander and lemon juice and season to taste with salt. Scatter coriander leaves over the curry and serve with rice and lemon wedges.

Slow-Cooker Risotto With Fennel, Lemon And Rocket

This vegetable risotto is gently cooked to perfection in the slow cooker, before being topped with Parmesan, fennel fronds and lemon zest.

Each serving provides 523 kcal, 12.5g protein, 75g carbohydrate (of which 4g sugars), 18g fat (of which 11g saturates), 4.5g fibre and 0.8g salt.

🍽 Servings: 4   🍲 Cooking Time: 2 Hours

Ingredients:

- 25g/1oz butter, diced
- 1 onion, finely chopped
- 2 large garlic cloves, sliced
- 1 large fennel bulb, trimmed and diced, green leaves reserved for garnish
- 1.4 litres/2½ pints hot vegetable stock
- 350g/12oz arborio rice
- 50g/1¾oz grated Parmesan, plus extra to serve (optional)
- 4 tbsp double cream
- 2 unwaxed lemons, zest of 2 and juice of 1
- 90g/3¼oz rocket leaves
- 10g basil leaves
- salt

Directions:

1. Preheat the slow cooker to the highest setting.
2. Place the butter, onion, garlic and fennel in the slow cooker. Pour in 1.1 litres/1¾ pints of the hot stock and cook for 2 hours, or until the fennel and onion are really soft.
3. Using a slotted spoon, transfer roughly half of the vegetables from the slow cooker to a food processor or blender. Blend, adding enough of the stock to create a really smooth, silky purée. Stir back into the slow cooker with the risotto rice. Cover and cook until the rice is tender and creamy. Start checking after 45 minutes, and if not ready, check every 5 minutes after that. It should be well cooked in an hour.
4. Turn off the slow cooker and stir the Parmesan and cream into the risotto. Stir in most of the lemon zest and the juice. If it's too thick, loosen with up to 200ml/7fl oz of the extra stock. If you need any extra liquid, just use boiling water.
5. Place half the rocket leaves into a food processor or blender with the final 100ml/3½fl oz of stock, the basil leaves and a good pinch of salt. Blend to a purée, scraping down the sides down a couple of times.
6. Swirl the rocket purée through the risotto and ladle into bowls. Serve topped with the remaining rocket leaves, lemon zest and fennel fronds – plus an extra grating of Parmesan, if you like.

Notes:

1. As this risotto is so delicately flavoured, add some extras if preferred. Frozen peas make a good vitamin-boosting addition for kids, toasted walnuts or pine nuts scattered on top elevate it to dinner party status.

Slow Cooker Chicken Pie Filling

This is planning ahead- cook this tasty slow-cooker chicken pie filling a day ahead so that it's ready for topping with all-butter puff pastry. Making pie as easy as... pie.

Servings: 4   **Cooking Time:** 2 Hours

Ingredients:

- 1 tsp vegetable oil
- 6 skinless, boneless chicken thighs (about 500g/1lb 2oz), cut into bite-sized pieces
- salt and freshly ground black pepper
- 3 medium leeks, trimmed
- 1 onion, chopped
- a few sprigs fresh thyme
- 1 tbsp butter
- 2 tbsp plain flour
- 350ml/12fl oz good-quality chicken stock
- 100g/3½oz good-quality ham, torn into bite-sized pieces
- 100g/3½oz crème fraîche, optional

Directions:

1. Heat the oil in a large non-stick frying pan. Season the chicken with salt and freshly ground black pepper and fry over a high heat for 10 minutes until golden-brown all over.
2. Meanwhile, slice the leeks into 1cm/½in rounds. Place the leeks, the onion and the thyme leaves into the slow cooker. Top with the chicken.
3. Add the butter to the pan, let it melt, then stir in the flour and cook for one minute or until pale gold and bubbling. Take the pan from the heat, then gradually whisk in the stock to make a smooth sauce. It will be very thick at first, but keep going. Pour the sauce over the chicken and vegetables, then cover and cook on low for 4 hours, or until the meat is very tender. Season with salt and freshly ground black pepper. Allow to cool, then chill.
4. Stir in the ham and the crème fraîche (if using) into the chilled chicken mixture and it's ready to top with shortcrust or puff-pastry. Bake in a hot oven for 40 minutes or until piping hot and golden brown.

Notes:

1. All fillings for pastry-topped pies need to be cooled before covering with pastry. Transfer the filling to a large, shallow container to cool the chicken as quickly as possible before chilling for up to two days, or freezing for up to a month.

Slow Cooker Chicken Pho

This slow cooker chicken noodle soup recipe makes a richly flavoured stock for its base you could use in other recipes, too.

Equipment and preparation: For this recipe, you will neeed a medium-sized electric slow-cooker. This meal provides 447 kcal, 58g protein, 43g carbohydrate (of which 3.5g sugars), 3g fat (of which 0.7g saturates), 1g fibre and 4g salt per portion.

Servings: 4   Cooking Time: 2 Hours

Ingredients:

- 1 onion, peeled, finely chopped
- 4 garlic cloves, halved
- 20g/¾oz fresh root ginger, peeled, thinly sliced
- 2 long fresh red chillies, sliced (or 1 tsp dried chilli flakes)
- 1 tsp Chinese five-spice powder
- 4 tbsp dark soy sauce, plus extra to serve
- 1kg-1.2kg/2lb 4oz-2lb 10oz whole chicken
- 1 tbsp Thai fish sauce (nam pla)
- 200g/7oz dried flat rice noodles
- To serve
- 6 spring onions, trimmed and thinly sliced
- 100g/3½oz beansprouts, rinsed and drained
- 25g/1oz fresh coriander sprigs
- 1 long red chilli, thinly sliced
- 1 lime, cut into wedges

Directions:

1. Place the vegetables in the slow-cooker. Stir in the five-spice powder, 1 litre/1¾ pints water and soy sauce until well combined.
2. Cut any string from the chicken, remove the skin by pushing your fingers between the breast meat and the skin and easing off the skin. Do the same with the legs, snipping off any skin around the wings or leg tips with scissors.
3. Place the chicken, breast-side up, in the slow-cooker, pushing it down among the vegetables. Season all over with salt and pepper.
4. Cover and cook on high for 4½ hours, or until the chicken is completely cooked through and very tender.
5. Drain the contents of the slow-cooker into a large bowl. Place the chicken on a chopping board and strip the meat from the carcass, thickly slice. Cover with foil.
6. Skim off the fat from the stock collected in the bowl using a large metal spoon. Pour the stock into a clean saucepan, stir in the fish sauce and place on a gentle simmer.
7. Half-fill a separate saucepan with water and bring to the boil. Add the noodles and cook until just tender, stirring regularly to separate them. Drain well.
8. Divide the noodles equally among 4 deep serving bowls. Top each with chicken, spring onions, beansprouts and coriander. Ladle over the hot stock and season with soy. Garnish with the remaining sliced chilli and lime wedges.

Notes:

1. Tip 1: Removing the skin from the chicken prevents the stock from becoming too fatty, but you can leave it on if preferred.
2. Tip 2: If you haven't got your timings quite right and the noodles are ready too early, run them under the cold tap and re-heat in the hot stock for 30 seconds just before serving.
3. Tip 3: Any leftover cooked chicken can be chilled in the fridge and used in sandwiches and salads.

Slow Cooker Chicken With Lemon And Olives

Enjoy this zesty Moroccan-style chicken with couscous, rice or flatbread - just keep an eye out for olive stones!

Servings: 4   Cooking Time: 2 Hours

Ingredients:

- 500g/1lb 2oz potatoes, halved then cut into 5cm/2in chunks
- salt and freshly ground black pepper
- 1 onion, sliced
- 4 whole chicken legs, each slashed four times on the skin side
- 1 tbsp vegetable oil
- 1 unwaxed lemon
- 2 fat garlic cloves, crushed
- 1 tbsp ras el hanout spice mix
- 400ml/14fl oz good quality chicken stock (or a mix of white wine and stock)
- 85g/3oz stone-in green olives in extra virgin olive oil (drained weight)
- 2 tsp clear honey
- handful fresh flat-leaf parsley
- Greek-style yogurt, to serve

Directions:

1. Place the potatoes and onions into a slow cooker and season with salt and freshly ground black pepper. Season the chicken generously. Heat the vegetable oil in a large frying pan then fry the chicken until golden-brown all over, about five minutes each side. Put the chicken on top of the vegetables.
2. Meanwhile, finely grate the zest of the lemon, cut four thin slices of lemon, then squeeze the juice from the rest of the fruit. Add the zest, garlic and ras el hanout to the chicken fat and juices, fry for a one minute till fragrant, then pour in the lemon juice and stock. Bring to the boil, then pour over the chicken. Top with the lemon slices, olives and one tablespoon olive oil from their jar, then cover with the lid and cook on low for six hours, until the chicken is very tender.
3. To serve, drizzle with the honey. Roughly chop the parsley leaves and scatter over the chicken. Serve with dollops of creamy yoghurt.

Notes:

1. If you can't find ras el hanout, use ½ tsp ground ginger, ½ tsp freshly ground black pepper, 1 tsp ground coriander and 1 tsp cinnamon instead.

Slow Cooker Beef Brisket With Bean Mash

This slow-cooker brisket recipe brings two of our favourite things together.: tender shreds of beef and easy slow cooking. This recipe requires no browning, but the stout makes the beef dark, rich and tender. A creamy bean mash is the perfect accompaniment.

If you are making this recipe to serve two, make half the mash as, unlike the beef, it won't freeze well. Equipment: you need a slow cooker and a blender to make this recipe.

Servings: 4   **Cooking Time: 2 Hours**

Ingredients:

- For the beef brisket
- 1.5kg/3lb 5oz beef brisket joint
- salt and freshly ground black pepper
- 2 onions, thinly sliced
- 3 fresh bay leaves
- 350ml/12fl oz Irish stout
- For the cannellini bean mash
- knob of butter
- 4 leeks, white parts only, thinly sliced
- 2 garlic cloves
- few sprigs fresh thyme, leaves only, or ½ tsp dried thyme
- 2 x 400g/14oz tins cannellini beans
- 4 tbsp crème fraîche
- 1 tbsp chopped fresh parsley (optional)

Directions:

1. Season the brisket joint generously with with salt and freshly ground black pepper.
2. Sprinkle the sliced onions and bay leaves over the bottom of the slow cooker, top with the brisket and pour over the stout.
3. Cook on low for 8-10 hours.
4. For the cannellini bean mash, heat the butter in a frying pan and cook the leeks over a very gentle heat for 20 minutes, or until completely softened.
5. Stir in the garlic and thyme leaves and season with salt and freshly ground black pepper.
6. Blend the beans, leek mixture, crème fraîche and parsley to a purée in a food processor or blender.
7. Return the mash to the frying pan and warm through. Season, to taste, with salt and freshly ground black pepper.
8. To serve, spoon the mash onto serving plates. Carve the brisket into slices and place alongside. Spoon over a little of the cooking liquid from the slow cooker.

Slow Cooker Coq Au Vin

This takes a little more effort than some slow cooker recipes but it's well worth the effort. Serve with good crusty bread or mashed potatoes.

Servings: 4   Cooking Time: 2 Hours

Ingredients:

- 400g/14oz shallots, peeled and left whole
- 2 carrots, cut into chunky pieces, about 2½cm/1in
- 2 sticks celery, cut into 1cm/½in slices
- salt and freshly ground black pepper
- 100g/3½oz smoked, dry-cured lardons
- 2 tbsp plain flour
- 4 whole chicken legs, cut into thighs and drumsticks
- 1 fresh bay leaf
- few sprigs fresh thyme, or 1 tsp dried
- 2 garlic cloves, crushed
- 1 tbsp tomato purée
- 300ml/½pt full-bodied red wine
- 100ml/3½fl oz good quality chicken stock
- 150g/5½oz button or crimini mushrooms, or larger mushrooms cut in half

Directions:

1. Put the shallots, carrots and celery into a slow cooker, and season with salt and freshly ground black pepper. Fry the lardons in a large frying pan over a low heat for 10 minutes until crisp, golden and the fat has run from the meat. Remove from the pan and tip most of the fat into a heatproof bowl.
2. Meanwhile, put the flour into a food bag or bowl, season with salt and freshly ground pepper, then toss the chicken pieces in the flour to coat.
3. Fry the floured chicken in the residual bacon fat until golden-brown, about five minutes each side. Put the chicken on top of the vegetables in the slow cooker and scatter with the lardons, bay leaf and thyme sprigs.
4. Add a little more fat to the pan if needed, then add the garlic and tomato purée. Cook for a minute, then add the wine and bring to the boil for two minutes. Add the stock, return to the boil, season with salt and freshly ground black pepper, then pour over the meat and vegetables. Cover with the lid then cook on low for six hours, until the chicken is very tender.
5. Just before serving, heat a little fat in a frying pan and fry the mushrooms over a high heat, until golden-brown. Scatter over the chicken and serve.

Notes:

1. Shallots can be time consuming to peel. To make it easier, pour boiling water over the shallots and let them soak for a few minutes. Drain, then peel. You will find that the skin comes away easily.

Slow Cooker Lamb Shanks

The meat on these lamb shanks is so tender that it falls off the bone. Serve with mounds of mash for the ultimate comfort food supper.

Servings: 4   Cooking Time: 2 Hours

Ingredients:

- 2 tbsp vegetable oil
- 4 lamb shanks
- 100g/3½oz plain flour, seasoned with salt and freshly ground black pepper
- 250ml/9fl oz red wine
- 1 onion, sliced
- 3 fresh sprigs rosemary
- 3 fresh bay leaves
- 300ml/½ pint chicken or vegetable stock
- mashed potatoes, to serve

Directions:

1. Heat the oil in a large frying pan.
2. Dredge the lamb shanks in the seasoned flour and fry in the frying pan for 4-5 minutes, turning regularly, or until browned all over. Place the lamb shanks in the slow cooker.
3. Deglaze the frying pan with the red wine and continue to cook for 2-3 minutes, or until the volume of the liquid has reduced by half. Pour the liquid into the slow cooker.
4. Add the onion, rosemary, bay leaves and stock to the slow cooker. The liquid should cover the meat - add more stock or boiling water if needed.
5. Cook on high for eight hours. Serve with mash.

Notes:

1. You'll need a large slow cooker to fit all of the lamb shanks in.
2. If you are cooking this recipe for two, the cooked lamb shanks will keep in the freezer for up to 4 weeks.

Slow-Cooker Spring Chicken And Herb Soup

An alternative option is to use a whole chicken instead of the thighs in this soup. Shred the leg and thigh meat as per the recipe and keep the breast meat for sandwiches.

Servings: 8   **Cooking Time: 2 Hours**

Ingredients:

- 4 large chicken thighs, bone in, skin and extra fat removed
- 2 onions, roughly chopped
- 1 tsp English mustard powder
- 2 chicken stock pots (or stock cubes)
- 2 tbsp wholegrain mustard
- 2 bay leaves
- 2.5 litres/4½ pints boiling water
- 300g/10½oz baby Chantenay carrots, scrubbed and larger ones halved
- 125g/4½oz pearl barley
- 200g/7oz frozen peas
- 200g/7oz frozen broad beans
- 15g/½oz fresh flatleaf parsley, finely chopped
- 10g fresh tarragon, finely chopped
- 10g fresh chives, finely snipped
- ½ lemon, juice only
- salt and freshly ground black pepper

Directions:

1. Preheat the slow cooker to the lowest setting and boil the kettle.
2. Put the chicken thighs and onions into the slow cooker with the mustard powder, stock pots, wholegrain mustard and bay leaves. Pour over the boiling water, put on the lid and leave to cook for 5 hours.
3. Stir in the carrots and pearl barley. Continue cooking for a further hour until the carrots and barley are tender.
4. Turn off the slow cooker and remove the chicken. Remove and discard the bay leaves, and stir in the peas and broad beans. Re-cover.
5. Shred the chicken meat from the bones into small pieces. Stir the chicken, herbs and lemon juice into the soup and season with salt and pepper. Ladle straight into bowls, or leave to cool to room temperature before chilling and reheating over the next day or two.

Notes:

1. You can always use normal carrots that have been cut into bitesize pieces.

Slow Cooker Beef Curry

Use your slow cooker for this simple beef curry - it's full of flavour and guarantees meltingly tender beef. Serve with rice and naan bread.

Each serving provides 334 kcal, 33g protein, 12g carbohydrates (of which 10g sugars), 16.5g fat (of which 5g saturates), 2g fibre and 0.3g salt.

Servings: 6   Cooking Time: 2 Hours

Ingredients:

- 4 tbsp sunflower oil
- 800g/1lb 12oz beef braising steak, cut into 2.5cm/1in pieces
- 2 onions, finely chopped
- 4 garlic cloves, finely chopped
- 2 chillies, finely chopped, plus extra to taste
- 2.5cm/1in piece fresh root ginger, peeled and finely grated
- 4 tsp ground cumin
- 4 tsp ground coriander
- 2 tsp ground turmeric
- 2 x 400g cans chopped tomatoes
- 2 tsp garam masala
- 200g/7oz natural yoghurt
- small handful fresh chopped coriander (optional)

Directions:

1. Heat half of the oil in a frying pan and fry the beef pieces for 4–5 minutes, or until browned all over. (You may need to brown the meat in batches.) Tip the browned meat into the slow cooker.
2. Heat the remaining oil in a frying pan and fry the onions for 5 minutes, then add the garlic, chilli and ginger and fry for another 2–3 minutes. Add the spices and fry for another minute, then tip the mixture into the slow cooker.
3. Add the chopped tomatoes to the slow cooker, then fill one of the empty cans with water and add the water to the slow cooker.
4. Stir everything together, pressing down so that everything is covered in liquid and cook for 8–10 hours on low.
5. About 30 minutes before serving, stir in the garam masala and yoghurt and season to taste with salt and a little more chilli. Cook for a further 30 minutes, then stir in the coriander.

Notes:

1. Alternatively, you can cook this curry on the hob for 2-3 hours on a low heat, or until the beef is very tender.

Slow Cooker Chicken Casserole With Dumplings

Adding dumplings to this simple, slow-cooker chicken casserole makes it great value when feeding the family.

Servings: 4   Cooking Time: 2 Hours

Ingredients:

- For the casserole
- 8 chicken thighs, skin on, bone in
- 2 tbsp sunflower oil
- 2 onions, thinly sliced
- 600g/1lb 5oz large waxy potatoes, peeled, cut into chunks
- 3 carrots, peeled, cut into chunks
- 2 parsnips, peeled, cut into chunks
- 3 tbsp plain flour
- 200ml/7fl oz hot chicken stock (made with 1 stock cube)
- 500ml/18fl oz dry cider
- 1 tbsp wholegrain mustard
- salt and freshly ground black pepper
- For the dumplings
- 200g/7oz self-raising flour, plus extra for dusting
- 100g/3½oz suet, shredded
- 3 tbsp finely chopped fresh sage (or 1 tsp dried sage leaves)

Directions:

1. Season the chicken thighs all over with a little salt and pepper. Heat the oil in a large, heavy-based, non-stick frying pan over a medium heat. Add the chicken thighs skin-side down and fry for 6-8 minutes, or until deep golden-brown.
2. Turn the chicken over and fry for 2-3 minutes. Transfer the chicken to a plate and set aside.
3. Put the vegetables in the slow-cooker. Sprinkle over the flour and stir to coat. Add the chicken and pour over the stock and cider. Stir in the mustard. Cover and cook on high for 4½ hours.
4. When the casserole has been cooking for about 4 hours, make the dumplings. Mix together the flour, suet and sage in a large mixing bowl. Season with salt and pepper.
5. Make a well and gradually pour in 125ml/4fl oz cold water in a thin stream, slowly bringing the dry ingredients into the pool of water and stirring using a wooden spoon until the mixture comes together as a soft, squidgy dough.
6. Turn the dough out onto a lightly floured work surface and divide it into 12 pieces. Roll the pieces into balls.
7. Remove the lid from the slow-cooker and skim off any fat that has risen to the surface. Arrange the dumplings on top of the casserole and cover. Cook for 30 minutes, or until the dumplings puff up.
8. Spoon the casserole and dumplings onto plates and serve with steamed kale, shredded cabbage or green beans.

Notes:

1. This casserole can be made with boneless, skinless chicken thighs if preferred, but the bone-in thighs add extra flavour.
2. To considerably reduce the calories and fat in this recipe, half the dumpling recipe to make eight dumplings (two smaller dumplings per person).

Slow Cooker Chicken And Vegetable Tagine

This healthy slow cooker tagine is the friend you want to see at the end of the day. You can even prepare it the night before and pop it in the fridge (in the slow cooker bowl) ready to cook in the morning. Serve with brown rice or whole wheat couscous.

Each serving provides 412 kcal, 26g protein, 38g carbohydrates (of which 22g sugars), 14g fat (of which 3g saturates), 15g fibre and 1.4g salt.

Servings: 4   Cooking Time: 2 Hours

Ingredients:

- 2 tbsp olive oil
- 2 onions, cut into chunks
- 2 garlic cloves, chopped
- 4 chicken thighs, skin on, bone in
- 1 tsp ground cumin
- 1 tsp smoked paprika
- 1 tsp ground coriander
- 1 tsp ground cinnamon
- 1 tsp ground ginger
- 4 carrots, cut into chunks
- 2 parsnips, cut into chunks
- 2 peppers (any colour), seeds removed, cut into chunks
- 1 tsp dried oregano
- 400g tin chopped tomatoes
- 400g tin chickpeas, drained and rinsed
- 1 tbsp tomato purée
- ½ lemon, juice only

Directions:

1. Heat the oil in a frying pan over a medium heat. Add the onions, garlic and chicken and fry for 5 minutes, or until the onions have softened and the chicken is golden. Stir in the spices and then transfer to the slow cooker.
2. Put the carrots, parsnips, peppers and oregano into the slow cooker. Pour in the chopped tomatoes, then half-fill the tin with water and add to the slow cooker. Add the chickpeas, tomato purée and lemon juice.
3. Cook on low for 5–7 hours. The chicken should be falling off the bone. You can serve it as is or remove the bones before serving, with brown rice or wholewheat couscous.

Easy Slow Cooker Beef Stew

An easy slow cooker beef stew that's ready when you are. Throw store cupboard ingredients into the slow cooker with some inexpensive braising steak and serve with mash.

Each serving (without mash) provides 293 kcal, 34g protein, 13g carbohydrates (of which 13g sugars), 11g fat (of which 4g saturates), 4g fibre and 2.5g salt.

Servings: 6   Cooking Time: 2 Hours

Ingredients:

- 600ml/20fl oz just-boiled water
- 1 beef stock cube
- 2 tbsp tomato purée
- 1 tbsp yeast extract
- 900g/2lb good-quality braising steak, trimmed and cut into roughly 4cm/1½in chunks
- 100g/3½oz smoked bacon lardons, or sliced smoked back bacon
- 2 onions, thinly sliced
- 4 carrots (about 400g/14oz), peeled and cut into roughly 3cm/1¼in chunks
- 4 celery sticks, trimmed and cut into roughly 3cm/1¼in lengths
- 3 tbsp plain flour (25g/1oz)
- 1 tsp flaked sea salt, plus extra to season
- 1 tsp dried mixed herbs
- 1 bay leaf (dried or fresh)
- ground black pepper
- mashed potatoes, to serve

Directions:

1. Pour the just-boiled water into a heatproof measuring jug, add the stock cube, tomato purée and yeast extract. Stir well until the cube has dissolved and set aside.
2. Put the beef, bacon and vegetables in a slow cooker, sprinkle over the flour and add the salt, herbs and plenty of freshly ground black pepper. Toss together. Add the stock mixture and stir well.
3. Cover with the lid and cook on low for 8–10 hours, until the beef and vegetables are tender. Serve the beef stew with mashed potatoes.

Notes:

1. Beef shin or beef brisket will also work in this stew. You can pack the slow cooker the night before and keep it in the fridge, but you must add cooled beef stock instead of hot. Take the packed slow cooker out of the fridge for 30 minutes before putting it on to reduce the risk of cracking the dish. The stew will take 10 hours if started from cold.

Slow Cooker Minestrone

This hearty Italian soup is made with pasta and beans. This minestrone is great for batch cooking, just divide into portions and pop in the freezer and wonderfully warming soup will never be far from your bowl.
Each serving provides 352kcal, 24g protein, 29g carbohydrate (of which 9.5g sugars), 14g fat (of which 4g saturates), 8.5g fibre and 1.5g salt.

Servings: 4   Cooking Time: 2 Hours

Ingredients:

- 100g/3½oz smoked, dry-cured lardons
- 2 carrots, roughly chopped
- 2 sticks celery, sliced
- 1 onion, roughly chopped
- 2 garlic cloves, crushed
- 2 sprigs fresh rosemary, needles finely chopped
- 1 tsp dried thyme
- 1 tbsp tomato purée
- 400g/14oz can chopped plum tomatoes
- 1.2 litres/2 pints good-quality chicken stock
- 400g/14oz can cannellini beans in water, rinsed and drained
- 50g/1¾oz spaghetti, snapped into short lengths
- 100g/3½ head baby leaf or spring greens, thickly shredded
- Salt and freshly ground black pepper
- 2 tbsp extra virgin olive oil
- 25g/1oz parmesan, grated (optional)

Directions:

1. Put a large frying pan over a low heat, add the lardons and cook for 10 minutes until crisp, golden and the fat has run from the meat. Transfer onto a plate.
2. Tip the carrots, celery and onion into the bacon fat and fry for two minutes before adding the garlic, herbs and tomato purée. Cook for 1 minute, then add the tomatoes and most of the stock. Bring to the boil. Carefully transfer the soup to a slow cooker, cover with the lid, then cook on high for 4 hours until the vegetables are tender.
3. Stir the beans and pasta into the soup, adding the rest of the stock if it seems overly thick. Scatter the shredded greens over the top of the soup, then re-cover with the lid. Cook for 30 minutes until the pasta is tender. Stir in the greens, season with salt and pepper, then serve in bowls with a drizzle of oil and plenty of parmesan.

Notes:

1. This soup will keep in the freezer for 2 months.

Slow Cooker Harissa Vegetable Stew

If you're worried about the levels of heat in this dish – and different brands of harissa can vary in heat – just add 2 tablespoons to start with. Then assess the spiciness at the end when you check the seasoning and add as little or much of the final tablespoon as preferred.

Servings: 6   Cooking Time: 2 Hours

Ingredients:

- 400g/14oz parsnips, trimmed, peeled, woody core removed and cut into short batons
- 2 onions, red, white or a mixture, cut into very thin wedges
- 4 large carrots, peeled and cut into 2cm/¾in slices
- 2 x 400g tins butterbeans (or other white beans)
- 3 tbsp harissa
- 1 tbsp dried oregano or mixed herbs
- 1 tbsp honey
- 400g tin chopped tomatoes
- 400ml/14fl oz vegetable stock
- 2 tbsp tomato purée
- about 100g/3½oz kale, thick stalks discarded and roughly chopped
- salt and freshly ground black pepper
- To serve
- freshly cooked couscous, rice or jacket potatoes
- plain yoghurt

Directions:

1. Turn the slow cooker to the high setting to heat up. Add the parsnips, onions and carrots. Drain one of the tins of butterbeans and tip into the slow cooker with the other tin of beans and its liquid. Add the harissa, oregano, honey, chopped tomatoes, stock and tomato purée. Season generously with salt and pepper and stir. Cook for 3–4 hours on high or 5–6 hours on low, until all of the vegetables are really tender.

2. Stir in the kale, cover the slow cooker with the lid and leave to soften for 5 minutes. Season with salt and pepper and serve with couscous, rice or jacket potatoes and dollops of yoghurt.

Slow Cooker Goulash

There's nothing nicer than coming home to a comforting meal – in this case, a beef goulash that's been bubbling away in your slow cooker! Serve with freshly cooked rice, jacket potatoes or tagliatelle, with some green vegetables alongside.

Each serving provides 563 kcal, 57g protein, 24g carbohydrates (of which 17g sugars), 25g fat (of which 9g saturates), 6g fibre and 1.1g salt.

Servings: 4 Cooking Time: 2 Hours

Ingredients:

- 3 tbsp olive oil
- 1kg/2lb 4oz braising or stewing beef, cut into chunks (see recipe tip below)
- 2 tbsp plain flour
- 1½ tbsp mild paprika (not smoked)
- 2 onions, chopped
- 2 garlic cloves, crushed
- 3 peppers, any colour, cut into bite-sized chunks
- 400g tin chopped tomatoes
- 2 tbsp tomato purée
- 1 tsp caraway seeds (optional)
- 1 beef stock cube, crumbled
- 1 tsp caster or granulated sugar
- salt and freshly ground black pepper
- ½ small bunch curly or flatleaf parsley, chopped, to garnish
- 8 tbsp soured cream, to serve

Directions:

1. Brown the beef the night before or in the morning. Heat 2 tablespoons of the oil in a large frying pan over a medium heat and fry the meat in batches, until the chunks are sealed and browned all over.
2. Remove the beef and place in a bowl. Pour 200ml/7fl oz water into the frying pan and bring to a simmer, scraping up all the beefy bits on the bottom. Tip into a jug. Stir the flour and paprika into the beef chunks. Put back into the pan with the remaining oil and cook, stirring, for 2 minutes until the dustiness has disappeared. If preparing the night before, cool the meat to room temperature then chill overnight with the jug of stock.
3. To cook the goulash, place the beef chunks, onions, garlic and peppers in the slow cooker. Tip the tomatoes into a large jug or bowl and stir through the tomato purée, caraway seeds, if using, crumbled stock cube and sugar. Pour 450ml/16fl oz water into the reserved stock and pour this stock mixture and the tomato mixture all over the beef and vegetables. Give everything a good stir.
4. Turn the slow cooker to low and cook for 7–9 hours until the beef is falling apart and tender and the sauce has thickened slightly. Season with salt and pepper and stir through half of the parsley. To serve, swirl through the soured cream and garnish with the remaining parsley and some black pepper.

Notes:

1. Pick a cut of meat to suit your schedule. Leaner, slow-cook cuts like silverside and brisket will be ready more quickly (in fact they will be a bit dry if cooked for too long), so are suited to 7 hour stews. Fattier, tougher cuts like shin, ox cheek, feather blade or chuck will melt down nicely over 9 hours.

Slow Cooker Chinese-Style Beef

This slow-cooker beef recipe makes a lovely change from a stir-fry but is just as easy to prepare.
Equipment and preparation: For this recipe, you will need an electric slow-cooker, at least 3.5 litres/6 pints in capacity.

Servings: 4   Cooking Time: 2 Hours

Ingredients:

- 2 tbsp sunflower oil
- 2 large red onions, thinly sliced
- 50g/1¾oz piece fresh root ginger, peeled, finely grated
- 4 garlic cloves, crushed
- 1 tsp dried chilli flakes
- 500g/1lb 2oz braising steak, trimmed, cut into 5cm/2in cubes
- 2 tsp Chinese five-spice powder
- 350ml/12fl oz hot beef stock (made with 1 stock cube)
- 4 tbsp dark soy sauce
- 4 tsp cornflour
- 2 tbsp clear honey
- freshly ground black pepper

Directions:

1. Heat the oil in a large, heavy-based frying pan over a medium heat. Add the onions and fry for 8-10 minutes, stirring regularly, until softened and lightly browned. Add the ginger, garlic and chilli flakes, stir well and cook for 2-3 minutes, making sure the garlic doesn't burn.
2. Season the beef all over with pepper, then sprinkle over the five-spice powder and mix to coat evenly. Add to the pan and fry for 3-4 minutes, turning the beef regularly until lightly browned all over.
3. Transfer to the slow-cooker. Pour over the stock and stir in the soy sauce. Cover and cook on high for 4 hours, until the beef is meltingly tender.
4. When the beef is cooked, whisk the cornflour with 1 tablespoon water to a smooth paste, stir in the honey. Add to the slow-cooker, cover and cook for 12-15 minutes, or until the sauce is glossy and has thickened slightly.
5. Serve the beef with steamed rice or boiled noodles and stir-fried vegetables.

Notes:

1. If you are using pre-cut beef, it will probably be in small chunks, so reduce the cooking time by about 1 hour. Also, If you are not using a slow cooker you may need to add extra beef stock.

Slow Cooker Meatballs In Tomato Sauce

Give the onions a quick fry before adding all the ingredients to the slow cooker to bubble away for most of the day. Serve the meatballs with tagliatelle and plenty of Parmesan.

Servings: 4   **Cooking Time: 2 Hours**

Ingredients:

- 1 tbsp olive oil
- 1 onion, finely chopped
- 1 garlic clove, crushed
- 400g/14oz can chopped tomatoes
- 2 tbsp tomato purée
- 1 tsp dried oregano or dried mixed herbs
- ¼ tsp dried chilli flakes (optional)
- 1 dried bay leaf
- 12 ready-made fresh beef mince meatballs (around 375g/13oz)
- salt and freshly ground black pepper
- To serve
- freshly cooked tagliatelle
- grated Parmesan

Directions:

1. Heat the oil in a small frying pan and fry the onion for 4–5 minutes, or until softened and lightly browned, stirring regularly. Add the garlic and cook for a few seconds more.
2. Transfer the cooked onion and garlic to a slow cooker and add the tomatoes, tomato purée, oregano (or dried mixed herbs), chilli (if using) and bay leaf.
3. Pour over 400ml/14fl oz of water, season with a good pinch of salt and lots of ground black pepper and stir well. Add the meatballs and turn to coat in the sauce.
4. Cover with a lid and cook on low for 10-12 hours or until the sauce is thick, the onion is softened and the meatballs are tender. Serve with freshly cooked tagliatelle, and sprinkled with plenty of grated Parmesan.

Slow Cooker Chicken Korma

This family-friendly curry is easily doubled, so you can make extra to store in the freezer for another dinner.

Servings: 4-5 **Cooking Time: 2 Hours**

Ingredients:

- 2 small–medium onions, roughly chopped
- 100g/3½oz korma curry paste (or follow pack guidance for serving 4–5 people)
- 2 tsp ground turmeric
- 40g/1½oz flaked almonds, plus 2 tbsp to garnish (toasted if preferred)
- 8 small chicken thighs (about 700–750g/1lb 9oz–1lb 10oz) skin removed, boneless, excess fat trimmed and each thigh cut into 3–5 pieces
- 100ml/3½fl oz double cream or Greek-style yoghurt
- handful sultanas or raisins (optional)
- salt and freshly ground black pepper
- freshly cooked basmati rice and/or warmed naan bread, to serve

Directions:

1. Turn the slow cooker to the High setting to heat up. Put the onions, curry paste, turmeric and flaked almonds into a food processor. Add 100ml/3½fl oz water then whizz until the paste is very smooth. Scrape the paste into the slow cooker.
2. Stir the chicken pieces into the paste mixture. Add another 200ml/7fl oz water and cook on Low for 6 hours or on High for 3 hours, until the chicken is really tender and the sauce is thick and golden.
3. Stir in the cream and sultanas, if using, and cook for another 15 minutes on High.
4. Taste the curry and season with salt and pepper. Scatter with the reserved flaked almonds and serve with rice or bread.

Slow Cooker Lamb Rogan Josh

If you're cooking for the family, this easy slow cooker lamb curry makes a feast with rice, extra yoghurt and cucumber for freshness. Make the curry even more special by scattering with pomegranate seeds or chopped coriander.

Servings: 4   Cooking Time: 2 Hours

Ingredients:

- 2 onions, 1½ roughly chopped, ½ thinly sliced
- 100g/3½oz rogan josh spice paste (or follow pack guidance for serving 4 people)
- 600g/1lb 5oz lamb neck fillet or shoulder, excess fat trimmed and diced into 3–4cm/1¼–1½in chunks
- 1½ tsp cumin seeds
- 1 cinnamon stick
- 2 fresh or dried bay leaves
- 400g tin plum tomatoes
- 1 pepper, any colour, cut into big chunks (optional)
- 100g/3½oz full-fat Greek-style or plain yoghurt
- salt and freshly ground black pepper
- freshly cooked rice, to serve

Directions:

1. Turn the slow cooker to the High setting to heat up. Put the roughly chopped onions and curry paste in a food processor with 100ml/3½fl oz water and whizz until smooth. Scrape into the slow cooker, then add the thinly sliced onion, lamb chunks, cumin seeds, cinnamon and bay leaves.

2. Use kitchen scissors to snip the plum tomatoes into small pieces inside the tin, then tip into the slow cooker. Give everything a good stir, season with salt and pepper and cover with the lid. Cook for 4 hours on High or 8–9 hours on Low until the lamb is tender, but not dry. If using the pepper, add for the last hour of cooking.

3. Stir in the yoghurt and leave for 10 minutes before serving. Taste and season again if needed and serve with rice or preferred serving options.

Notes:

1. Use a tin of chopped tomatoes if that is all you have, but whole tomatoes are often cheaper and make a richer sauce that is good for a curry.

2. Ready-made pastes are a great kitchen shortcut, so if you liked this recipe then it is very easily adapted to create other curries.

3. Tikka masala: use tikka masala paste, leave out the cinnamon stick and swap the yoghurt for double cream. Serve sprinkled with coriander.

4. Jalfrezi: use jalfrezi paste, swap the cinnamon stick for a whole green chilli and leave out the yoghurt. Season with a squeeze of lemon juice and use a green pepper.

5. Madras: use 200ml/7fl oz coconut milk instead of the water when whizzing the paste and swap the rogan josh for madras paste. Leave out the cinnamon and bay leaves, adding a few curry leaves instead if you have any.

Slow Cooker Dal

Tasty and filling, dal makes a cheap, healthy and satisfying meal. Try freezing it in portion-sized containers - it will keep for up to 2 months. Each serving provides 356kcal, 19g protein, 46g carbohydrate (of which 6g sugars), 9g fat (of which 1g saturates), 8g fibre and 1g salt.

Servings: 4   **Cooking Time: 2 Hours**

Ingredients:

- 300g/10½oz yellow split peas
- 1 onion, chopped
- 200g/7oz chopped tomatoes (from a tin or fresh)
- thumb of fresh root ginger, finely grated
- 2 tsp cumin seeds, 1 tsp crushed finely in a mortar
- 2 tsp ground turmeric
- 2 garlic cloves, one crushed, one thinly sliced
- 10 freeze-dried curry leaves
- 700ml/1¼ pts hot vegetable stock
- 1 hot green finger chilli, thinly sliced
- 2 tbsp vegetable or sunflower oil
- lemon wedges, to serve

Directions:

1. Place the split peas, onion, tomatoes, ginger, ground cumin, turmeric, crushed garlic, curry leaves and stock into a slow cooker. Add most of the chilli and stir to combine. Cook on high for four hours, until the split peas are tender.

2. Season the dal generously with salt and freshly ground black pepper. Just before serving, heat the oil in a saucepan. When the oil is very hot, add the whole cumin seeds and the sliced garlic. Fry until the garlic is golden-brown and the cumin smells toasty and almost smoky. Spoon the hot spiced oil over the dhal, scatter with the remaining green chilli, then serve with lemon wedges for squeezing.

Slow Cooker Beef Bourguignon

Although beef bourguignon is traditionally considered a decadent dish, by increasing the vegetable content slightly and reducing the beef, it can be both delicious and budget friendly. The low and slow cooking technique is also ideal for cheaper cuts of meat.

Servings: 6 **Cooking Time: 2 Hours**

Ingredients:

- 1kg/2lb 4oz braising beef, such as shin, cheek, brisket or stewing or chuck steak, cut into 4–5cm/1½– 2in chunks
- 250g/9oz shallots, peeled and larger ones halved
- 5 garlic cloves, 4 halved, 1 crushed
- 200g/7oz bacon lardons or smoked streaky bacon, sliced into strips
- 4–5 large carrots, peeled and each cut into 3–4 chunks
- about 6 fresh thyme sprigs
- 3 tbsp plain flour
- 3 tbsp tomato purée
- 1 beef stock pot or stock cube, crumbled
- 375ml/13fl oz cooking red wine
- 15g/½oz butter
- 125g/4½oz button mushrooms, larger ones halved or all thickly sliced if preferred
- salt and freshly ground black pepper
- 1 tbsp cornflour (optional)
- freshly steamed green vegetables and creamy mashed potato, to serve

Directions:

1. Turn the slow cooker to the High setting to heat up. Add the beef to the slow cooker with the shallots, halved garlic cloves, bacon, carrot and thyme sprigs.
2. Mash together the flour, tomato purée and stock pot or cube in a large bowl, then gradually stir in 300ml/10fl oz water. Stir into the beef and vegetables with the red wine. Cover and cook on Low for 7–8 hours or High for about 5 hours, depending on the cut used (see Tips below).
3. When the casserole is almost ready, heat the butter in a frying pan and fry the mushrooms until golden brown and softened. Stir in the crushed garlic and cook for 1–2 minutes. Stir the mushroom mixture into the slow cooker.
4. If you want the sauce to be a little thicker, mix a splash of the sauce from the slow cooker with the cornflour to create a smooth paste in the mushroom frying pan. Gradually stir in another ladleful of the sauce and cook, stirring over a medium heat, until it thickens dramatically. Stir this back into the slow cooker. Taste and season with salt and pepper. Serve the bourguignon with green vegetables and creamy mashed potatoes.

Notes:

1. Pick a cut of meat to suit your budget or schedule. Cuts that are leaner like brisket and silverside are suited to less cooking as they easily dry out, so cook on Low for 7 hours. Fattier, tougher cuts like cheek, shin, chuck and oxtail will take a bit longer but the added fat will result in a richer flavour.

Veggie Slow Cooker Curry

Just a few minutes precooking and this rich tasting slow-cooker veg curry can be quickly assembled – serve with basmati rice, plain yoghurt and assorted chutneys and pickles.

Each serving provides 248 kcal, 6g protein, 38g carbohydrates (of which 16.5g sugars), 6.5g fat (of which 0.5g saturates), 7.5g fibre and 1.6g salt.

Servings: 4   Cooking Time: 2 Hours

Ingredients:

- 1 tbsp sunflower oil
- 1 onion, thinly sliced
- 2 garlic cloves, very thinly sliced
- 3 tbsp Indian medium curry paste, such as tikka masala or rogan josh
- 2 tbsp plain flour
- 500g/1lb 2oz butternut squash, peeled and cut into roughly 2cm/¾in chunks
- 1 carrot, peeled, halved lengthways and cut into roughly 1cm/½in slices
- 400g/14oz can chopped tomatoes
- 400g/14oz can chickpeas, drained and rinsed
- 200g/7oz frozen spinach
- 1 tsp soft light brown sugar
- 400ml/14fl oz hot vegetable stock (made with 1 stock cube)
- freshly cooked basmati rice, plain or soya yoghurt and assorted chutneys and pickles

Directions:

1. Heat the oil in a large frying pan and gently fry the onion for 5 minutes, or until lightly browned, stirring frequently. Add the garlic and curry paste and cook for 30 seconds more, stirring constantly.
2. Transfer to the slow cooker and add the butternut squash and carrot. Sprinkle over the flour and toss together. Add the tomatoes, chickpeas, frozen spinach, sugar and stock.
3. Stir well, cover with the lid and cook on low for 9–11 hours, or until the vegetables are tender and the spices have mellowed. Stir well before serving with freshly cooked basmati rice, yoghurt and assorted chutneys and pickles.

Slow Cooker Mulligatawny Soup

This hearty, spiced soup makes for an easy meat-free Monday option. Frozen vegetable mixes are perfect for using in slow cookers. There's no need to defrost them first and no early morning chopping, as it's already been done for you.

Servings: 4   Cooking Time: 2 Hours

Ingredients:

- 1kg/2lb 4oz frozen or fresh casserole vegetable mix (containing root vegetables such as carrot, swede, turnip, onion and celery)
- 1½ tbsp mild curry powder
- 2 chicken or vegetable stock cubes
- 250g/9oz packet microwave pilau rice
- 15g/½oz fresh coriander
- salt and freshly ground black pepper
- 6 slices wholemeal bread, to serve

Directions:

1. Boil the kettle. Put the casserole vegetable mix in the slow cooker pot with the curry powder. Crumble in the stock cubes, season with pepper and then pour in 1.1 litres/2 pints boiling water from the kettle. Cover with the lid and cook on low for 8 hours until the vegetables are really tender.
2. Use a potato masher to mash the vegetables thoroughly in the pot until it forms a chunky soup. (If you prefer a slightly creamier finish, blend about a quarter of the soup with a stick blender, blender or food processor and stir back into the remaining soup.)
3. Crumble the rice into the soup to break up any lumps, then stir and leave to warm through for about 10 minutes. Finely chop most of the coriander, reserving some small leaves to garnish, and stir it through.
4. Season to taste with salt and pepper, divide between bowls and sprinkle over the reamining coriander leaves. Serve with the bread for dunking.

Notes:

1. Any leftovers can be frozen for up to 3 months.
2. If your supermarket doesn't stock the casserole vegetable mix, swap for 400g/14oz diced potatoes plus 600g/1lb 5oz frozen carrot, bean, pea and sweetcorn mix.

Slow Cooker Honey Roast Ham

How to cook ham in the slow cooker with zero effort. Then get it in the oven, slathered in mustard, honey and sugar, to crisp up. Irresistible.

Each serving provides 348 kcal, 37g protein, 5g carbohydrates (of which 5g sugars), 20g fat (of which 6.5g saturates), 0g fibre and 4.7g salt.

Servings: 10   Cooking Time: 2 Hours

Ingredients:

- 1.6kg/3lb 8oz boneless, rolled smoked or unsmoked gammon
- 1 onion, peeled and quartered
- 1 tbsp English mustard
- 1 tbsp clear honey
- 2 tbsp demerara sugar

Directions:

1. Put the gammon, onion and 100ml/3½fl oz water in the slow cooker, cover with the lid and cook on low for 6–8 hours, or until the pork is thoroughly cooked. The longer the gammon is cooked, the more like pulled ham it will become.
2. Remove the lid, lift the pork out of the slow cooker and onto a board, and leave it to stand for 10 minutes, or until cool enough to handle.
3. Preheat the oven to 220C/200C Fan/Gas 7. Very carefully, snip off the string and slide a knife, in a horizontal sawing motion, between the ham rind and fat, then lift off the rind, leaving a thin layer of fat on the meat. (You may need to do this in strips.)
4. Lightly score the ham fat with a knife in a crisscross pattern. Line a small roasting tin with a piece of foil, large enough to come up the sides of the tin. Place the ham on top, fat-side up. If the ham is thinner one end than the other, prop the short end up with a wodge of crumpled kitchen foil, so the fat is more horizontal – this will help it brown more evenly.
5. Mix the mustard, honey and sugar in a small bowl and spread it all over the ham fat. Bring the foil in towards the ham to create a bowl to catch any sticky juices. Bake the ham for 12–15 minutes, or until the fat is nicely browned.
6. Serve in slices, warm or cold.

Notes:

1. The cooking time in this recipe will give you slicing ham. If you would like a pulled pork style texture that brakes into strands, cook for 10 hours.

Slow Cooker Chicken Shawarma

This recipe features smoky, charred onions, grilled quickly at the end to serve with the spiced, slow-cooked chicken. The onions are a clever way to add a charred flavour that you might be missing from the meat.

Servings: 6-8   Cooking Time: 2 Hours

Ingredients:

- 1–1.2kg/2lb 4–10oz, about 10–12 chicken thighs, skin removed and boneless
- 4 garlic cloves, crushed
- 1 large lemon, juice only
- 3 tbsp olive oil
- 2–3 large onions, very thickly sliced into rounds
- few pinches dried oregano
- salt and freshly ground black pepper
- For the spice mix
- 2 tsp ground cumin
- 2 tsp ground coriander
- 2 tsp paprika (plain or sweet smoked, not hot)
- 2 tsp turmeric
- ½ tsp freshly ground black pepper
- ½ tsp cayenne pepper
- 2 tsp onion granules (optional)
- 1 tsp salt
- To serve
- warmed pitta, flatbread or wraps
- chopped salad ingredients
- tzatziki, hummus, garlic or chilli sauces
- pickled turnips and chilli

Directions:

1. Marinate the chicken overnight for best results. Mix together the spice mix ingredients in a food bag or bowl then sprinkle the spices over the chicken thighs. Use your hands to massage the spices all over the meat. Cover and leave in the fridge overnight or for as long as you have time for.

2. Turn the slow cooker to the high setting to heat up. In a jug, whisk the garlic, lemon juice and olive oil with a fork. Drizzle a bit in the base of the slow cooker and then add the chicken. Arrange the thighs at angles to fit in snugly and to create an even layer with no gaps. Drizzle the rest of the lemony oil over the top. Cook on low for 6 hours or on high for 3 hours, until the chicken is falling apart and still juicy.

3. Turn the slow cooker off and preheat the grill. Lay the onion rounds on a baking tray, brush the tops with some of the juices from the slow cooker, season with salt and pepper and sprinkle with half of the oregano. Flip the onions over and repeat. Grill for 2–4 minutes on each side until the onions are well charred.

4. Use two forks to shred the chicken. Place the shredded chicken inside the warmed breads with the charred onions, salads items, sauces and pickles.

Slow Cooker Chicken Noodle Soup

Nourishing, aromatic and deeply flavourful, this deceptively simple chicken soup makes the perfect family supper – best of all, there's hardly any washing up.

Servings: 4   Cooking Time: 2 Hours

Ingredients:

- 20g/¾oz fresh coriander, stalks finely chopped and leaves roughly chopped
- 6 chicken thighs, bone in and skinless
- 1 tbsp Chinese five-spice powder
- 4 tbsp soy sauce
- 100g/3½oz shiitake mushrooms, trimmed and roughly torn
- 20g/¾oz fresh root ginger, peeled and finely grated
- 4 spring onions, finely sliced
- 2 medium garlic cloves, finely grated
- 2 tbsp sesame oil
- 1 fresh red or green chilli, finely sliced (optional)
- 200g/7oz dried egg noodles
- 2 small pak choi (approx. 350g/12oz), shredded into 1cm/½in wide pieces
- salt and freshly ground black pepper

Directions:

1. Place the coriander stalks, chicken thighs, five-spice, soy sauce, shiitake mushrooms, half of the grated ginger, half of the spring onions and 1.2 litres/2 pints cold water into a slow cooker. Season with salt and pepper and stir to combine.
2. Cook on low for 4 hours or high for 2 hours. There is no need to open the lid and stir during the cooking time.
3. By the end, the chicken should be cooked through and tender with a rich and flavourful broth. Remove the chicken and replace the lid. Once the chicken is cool enough to handle, discard the bones and shred the meat before returning it to the slow cooker.
4. Around 5–10 minutes before you want to serve, add the remaining spring onions, coriander leaves and ginger, along with the garlic, sesame oil and chilli, if using. Stir well and check the seasoning, adding another splash of soy sauce if more salt is needed.
5. Add the noodles, submerging them evenly. Cook for a further 5–10 minutes with the lid on, checking after 5 minutes, until just cooked through.
6. Stir through the pak choi cover with the lid and leave to stand for a further minute before serving.

Notes:

1. Don't be tempted to open the lid during cooking. This lowers the temperature inside and increases the cooking time.

Slow Cooker Chipotle Pulled Pork

This slow cooker pulled pork recipe is great for feeding a crowd. It's so easy people won't believe how little effort it takes. Get a really good chipotle sauce if you want a bit of heat.

Servings: 4-6 **Cooking Time: 2 Hours**

Ingredients:

- 1.5kg/3lb 5oz pork shoulder
- 2 tbsp chipotle sauce
- For the fresh tomato salsa
- 6 tomatoes, chopped
- ½ red onion, finely chopped
- 1 tbsp lime juice (about ½ lime)
- small handful chopped fresh coriander
- ½ garlic clove, finely chopped
- 1 tsp olive oil
- For the guacamole
- 2 avocados, peeled, chopped
- ½ garlic clove, finely chopped
- 1 tbsp lime juice (about ½ lime), plus more to taste
- salt and freshly ground black pepper
- 12-16 flour tortillas, to serve

Directions:

1. Season the pork shoulder with salt. Place the pork shoulder into a slow cooker and cook on low for 8-10 hours.
2. Meanwhile, for the fresh tomato salsa, mix all of the ingredients together in a bowl and season, to taste, with salt, freshly ground black pepper and more lime juice.
3. For the guacamole, mash the avocado pieces and garlic together until smooth, then stir in the lime juice and season, to taste, with salt, freshly ground black pepper and more lime juice.
4. To serve, remove the skin and fat from the pork shoulder and shred the meat with two forks. Place the meat into a bowl. Mix the chipotle sauce with two tablespoons of the cooking liquid and pour the mixture over the pulled pork. Mix until the pork is coated in the sauce.
5. To serve, arrange the pork on a serving plate and spoon the salsa and guacamole into separate bowls. Warm the tortillas according to packet instructions and serve alongside.

Slow Cooker Chicken Cacciatore

This traditional chicken stew is rich and full flavoured, with classic Italian ingredients such as the herbs and olives. Adding lots of vegetables means only a small amount of meat is needed per person, but the sauce is generous so if you want to stretch it a bit further, just add a few more chicken thighs.

Servings: 6   Cooking Time: 2 Hours

Ingredients:

- 2 onions, finely chopped
- 2 celery sticks, finely chopped
- 6 garlic cloves, sliced
- 6 large boneless chicken thighs, skin removed
- 2 red, orange or yellow peppers, cut into big chunks
- 2 x 400g tins chopped tomatoes
- 150ml/5fl oz chicken stock, made with 1 stock cube
- 2 tsp dried basil
- 1 tbsp sugar
- 1 tbsp wine or balsamic vinegar
- 75g/2¾oz olives, stones removed and drained
- salt and freshly ground black pepper
- To serve
- freshly cooked pasta, potatoes or cheesy polenta
- freshly cooked green vegetables or salad

Directions:

1. Turn the slow cooker to the High setting to heat up. Add all of the ingredients with a really good grinding of fresh black pepper and some salt.
2. Cook on High for 3 hours or Low for 6 hours until the chicken is really tender. As it cooks, the meat should have broken down into smaller chunks but, if not, break the thighs into pieces with a spoon.
3. Serve with pasta, potatoes or cheesy polenta and green vegetables or salad.

Slow Cooker Lentil Soup

This simple soup can be made overnight for a tasty lunch the next day. It's hearty and filling, packed with nutritious ingredients. Want to keep it vegan? Just forego the cheese topping.

Servings: 4-6   Cooking Time: 2 Hours

Ingredients:

- 1 tbsp olive or vegetable oil
- 2 leeks, trimmed, cut in half vertically and sliced into 2cm/¾in strips
- 3 carrots, peeled and finely diced
- 2 celery stalks, finely diced
- 400g/14oz baby potatoes, quartered
- 150g/5½oz dried red lentils
- 400g tin chopped tomatoes
- 1.25 litres/2¼ pints vegetable stock
- 6 thyme sprigs, leaves picked
- 2 bay leaves
- salt and freshly ground black pepper
- grated Italian-style hard cheese, to serve (optional)

Directions:

1. Heat the oil in a large frying pan over a medium heat and add the leeks. Cook, stirring occasionally, for 5–7 minutes until softened then transfer to the slow cooker.
2. Add the carrots, celery, potatoes, lentils, tomatoes, stock, thyme and bay leaves. Cover with the lid and cook on low for 7–8 hours, until the lentils are soft.
3. Taste and season with salt and pepper. Remove and discard the bay leaves before dividing the soup between warmed bowls. Serve with a sprinkle of grated cheese on top, if using.

Slow Cooker Vegan Bean Chilli

Get this vegan chilli going in the slow cooker and you'll come back to a comforting dish to enjoy with rice, avocado, dairy-free yoghurt, coriander and lime wedges. A cheap, comforting dinner.

Each serving provides 332 kcal, 12.5g protein, 57g carbohydrate (of which 21g sugars), 1g fat (of which 0.5g saturates), 15g fibre and 0.7g salt.

Servings: 4   Cooking Time: 2 Hours

Ingredients:

- 8 spring onions, trimmed and thinly sliced
- 450g/1lb sweet potato, peeled and cut into roughly 2cm/¾in chunks
- 1 yellow pepper, seeds removed, finely chopped
- 2 garlic cloves, crushed
- ¼–½ tsp dried chilli flakes, depending on taste
- 1 tsp ground cumin
- 1 tsp ground coriander
- ½ cinnamon stick or ¼ tsp ground cinnamon
- 1 tbsp soft brown sugar
- 150ml/5fl oz hot vegetable stock (made with 1 vegan vegetable stock cube)
- 400g tin chopped tomatoes
- 395g tin red kidney beans in chilli sauce
- 400g tin mixed beans, drained and rinsed
- 1 tsp dried mixed herbs
- salt and ground black pepper
- To serve
- freshly cooked rice
- sliced avocado
- dairy-free yoghurt
- fresh coriander
- lime wedges

Directions:

1. Put all the ingredients into a slow cooker. Stir well then cover with the lid and cook on HIGH for 3–4 hours or LOW for 8–10 hours, or until the sauce is thick, the sweet potato is tender and the spices have mellowed.
2. If you get a chance, stir the chilli halfway through the cooking time, quickly replacing the lid.
3. Serve with freshly cooked rice, sliced avocado, dairy-free yoghurt, fresh coriander and lime wedges for squeezing.

Slow Cooker Beef Casserole

A slow cooker beef casserole recipe you'll make time and time again - no browning required! We've added a little orange peel, black olives, bay and red wine for a Provençal flavour.

Servings: 4   Cooking Time: 2 Hours

Ingredients:

- 500g/1lb 2oz braising steak, brisket or shin of beef cut into 2cm/1in chunks
- 150ml/5fl oz red wine
- 3 garlic cloves
- 2 medium onions, sliced
- 1 strip orange peel
- 1 bay leaf
- 1 tsp olive oil
- 100g/3½oz smoked bacon lardons
- 2 carrots, sliced
- 1 tbsp chopped parsley
- handful black olives
- salt and freshly ground black pepper

Directions:

1. Put the beef into a large bowl with the red wine, peeled garlic cloves, sliced onions, orange peel and bay leaf. Season with salt and pepper and give it all a stir. Cover the bowl with cling film and refrigerate for 30 minutes or overnight if cooking in the morning.
2. In the morning, add the olive oil to the bottom of the slow cooker with the bacon lardons. Tip half the beef and its marinade into the slow cooker. Add in the carrots, then tip the rest of the beef on top. Put the lid on the slow cooker and cook on high for 8-10 hours.
3. When ready to serve, stir in the chopped parsley and black olives. Serve the casserole with creamy mash or rice.

Notes:

1. If you prefer a thicker sauce for this slow cooker beef casserole, combine a tablespoon of flour with a tablespoon of butter, mashing together with a fork until completely combined. Take a mugful of the cooking juices out of the slow cooker and bring to the boil in a small saucepan. Add the butter mixture and simmer, stirring, until it is melted and the sauce is thickened. Return the thickened gravy to the slow cooker and stir throughout.

Slow Cooker Chicken Stew

This creamy slow cooker chicken stew is cheap, filling and healthy too. Serve with couscous or mash. Each serving provides 316kcal, 21g protein, 20g carbohydrate (of which 4.5g sugars), 14g fat (of which 4g saturates), 2.5g fibre and 0.6g salt.

Servings: 4-6   Cooking Time: 2 Hours

Ingredients:

- 100g/3½oz plain flour
- 4 tbsp sunflower oil
- 500g/1lb 2oz boneless, skinless chicken thigh, chopped into 2.5cm/1in pieces
- 1 onion, finely chopped
- 4 garlic cloves, finely chopped
- 2 chillies, finely chopped
- 175ml/6fl oz white wine
- ½ butternut squash, peeled, chopped into 2.5cm/1in pieces
- 300ml/10fl oz chicken stock
- 5 sprigs fresh thyme
- 3 bay leaves
- 4 tbsp crème fraîche
- small handful chopped fresh parsley
- salt and freshly ground black pepper

Directions:

1. Heat half of the oil in a frying pan. Sprinkle the flour onto a plate, and dredge the chicken pieces in the flour and fry for 4–5 minutes, or until browned all over. (You may need to brown the chicken in batches.) Tip the browned chicken into the slow cooker.
2. Heat the remaining oil in a frying pan and fry the onion for five minutes, then add the garlic and chilli and fry for another 2–3 minutes. Add the wine and continue to cook for another few minutes, or until the volume of the liquid is reduced by half.
3. Tip the onion mixture into the slow cooker. Add the butternut squash, chicken stock, thyme and bay leaves to the slow cooker. Stir everything together, pressing down so that everything is covered in liquid. Cook for 8–10 hours on low.
4. About 30 minutes before serving, stir in the crème fraîche and season to taste with salt and freshly ground black pepper. Cook for a further 30 minutes, then stir in the parsley.

Notes:

1. The stew can be cooked on the hob on low for 45 minutes to one hour, or until the chicken and butternut squash are tender. Stir in the crème fraîche and simmer for a further 10 minutes.

Slow Cooker Satay Chicken Wraps

If you like fajitas then you'll love this satay-style chicken version with pickled onions. And if you've only used your slow cooker for saucy stews before, you'll be so impressed by how easy it is to cook something like this pulled chicken dish instead.

Servings: 4 **Cooking Time: 2 Hours**

Ingredients:

- 200g/7oz salted, roasted peanuts
- 2 tbsp mild curry powder
- 1 lime, zest and juice
- 4 chicken legs, bone in and skin removed (about 1kg/2lb 4oz), or the same weight of chicken thighs
- 1 red onion, very finely sliced into rings (use a mandolin if you have one)
- 1 cucumber, halved lengthways then diagonally sliced
- 1 carrot, sliced into ribbons with a peeler then halved lengthways
- 8 soft white or wholemeal wraps

Directions:

1. Boil the kettle. Put 100g/3½oz peanuts in a small ceramic bowl, such as a cereal bowl. Pour over 150ml/5fl oz boiling water and leave the peanuts to soak for 30 minutes.
2. Reserving the water, drain the peanuts. Use a rolling pin, glass bottle or pestle and mortar to crush the peanuts to a fine crumble – do this in batches of 2–3 tablespoons at a time for ease.
3. Return all the crushed peanuts to the bowl with the reserved soaking water and mix in the curry powder, all the lime zest and half of the juice to create a chunky paste. (Alternatively, whizz the soaked peanuts, soaking water, curry powder, zest and juice in a mini food processor or blender to a paste.)
4. Put the paste and chicken legs in the slow cooker pot and, using your hands, rub the paste all over the chicken. Cover with the lid and cook on low for 7–8 hours, turning the legs over halfway through, until the meat is really tender and falling off the bones.
5. Half an hour before the end of the cooking time, place the onion slices in a bowl. Squeeze over the remaining lime juice and add some salt. Mix well and leave to pickle for 30 minutes, stirring occasionally.
6. Turn the slow cooker off and lift all of the meat and bones out of the sauce. Use forks to shred the meat into large chunks and discard the bones and any remaining skin. Stir a little of the satay sauce back through the chicken to moisten and put any remaining sauce into a serving bowl.
7. Place the cucumber slices, carrot ribbons, pickled onions and satay chicken on serving plates. Roughly chop the remaining peanuts and place in a small bowl. Warm the wraps according to packet instructions. Let everyone stuff their wraps with the choice of fillings and extra satay sauce before rolling up and eating.

Notes:

1. Extra lime wedges and sweet chilli sauce make great additions if you have any.
2. Leftover satay chicken can be frozen for up to 2 months. Pickles and salad will stay crunchy for 3 days in the fridge.

Slow Cooker Roast Beef Stew

This simple stew has a gravy-like sauce that benefits from browning the beef first, but you can also just throw everything in the slow cooker pot and it will still taste great. The Yorkshire puddings are included in the budget but are optional as they need to be cooked in an oven or air fryer, albeit only briefly.

Servings: 4 **Cooking Time: 2 Hours**

Ingredients:

- 2 tsp vegetable, sunflower or rapeseed oil
- 400–500g/14oz–1lb 2oz beef skirt, braising steaks or diced beef, chopped into 4–5cm/1½ –2in chunks
- 1 onion, sliced
- 4 tbsp gravy granules
- 2 tbsp wholegrain mustard
- 1 beef stock cube, crumbled
- 350g/12oz carrots, peeled and cut into 2–3cm/¾–1¼in batons
- 600g/1lb 5oz potatoes, peeled and cut into 4–5cm/1½ –2in chunks
- 12 frozen Yorkshire puddings (optional)
- 400g/14oz frozen peas
- salt and freshly ground black pepper

Directions:

1. Heat 1 teaspoon oil in a heavy-based frying pan. Divide the beef into two batches and add the first batch to the pan. Turn the beef to sear and colour on all sides to a rich, dark brown. Transfer the browned chunks straight to the slow cooker pot. Repeat with the remaining oil and beef.

2. Add the onion, gravy granules, mustard and stock cube to the pot and pour in 550ml/1 pint water. Give everything a quick stir, then add the carrots and potatoes. Cover with the lid and cook for 7 hours on low. Stir once during cooking, if you are at home, to rotate the meaty chunks sitting on the top.

3. Meanwhile, cook the Yorkshire puddings (if using) according to packet instructions or in an air fryer at 190C for 4 minutes. Steam, microwave or boil the peas for 3–4 minutes until cooked.

4. Season the stew with salt and pepper. Ladle portions of the stew onto plates and top with the Yorkshire puddings. Serve the green peas alongside.

Notes:

1. Any leftovers can be frozen for up to 3 months.
2. For ease, you can simply stir the peas through the stew in the slow cooker pot and cook on low for a final 10 minutes instead of serving them seperately.

Slow Cooker Chilli Con Carne

This slow cooker chilli recipe has a little hit of chocolate for a richness. It uses beef brisket, but you can also use braising steak or even beef mince if that's what you have.

Servings: 6 **Cooking Time: 2 Hours**

Ingredients:

- 1 onion, sliced
- 1 red pepper, deseeded and thickly sliced
- small bunch fresh coriander, stalks finely chopped
- 1 tbsp sunflower oil
- 500g/1lb 2oz beef brisket, trimmed of excess fat and cut into matchbox-size pieces
- salt and freshly ground black pepper
- 2 fat garlic cloves, crushed
- 1 tsp ground cumin
- 1 tsp ground coriander
- 2 tsp hot chilli powder
- 1 tsp dried oregano
- 2 tbsp tomato purée
- 400g/14oz can chopped tomatoes
- 300ml/½ pint hot beef stock
- 2 x 400g/14oz can red kidney beans in water, rinsed and drained
- 1 cube good quality dark chocolate, minimum 70% cocoa solids

Directions:

1. Place the onion, red pepper and coriander stalks into a slow cooker.
2. Heat the oil in a large non-stick frying pan, season the beef with salt and freshly ground black pepper, then fry in two batches until golden-brown, transferring to the slow cooker when ready.
3. Add the garlic, spices and oregano to the pan juices and fry for one minute until fragrant. Stir in the tomato purée, tomatoes and stock then bring to a boil. Pour the hot sauce over the beef in the slow cooker, then cover with a lid and cook on low for seven hours. Stir in the beans, then cook the chilli for an hour more until the meat is very tender.
4. Pop the chocolate into the chilli, let it melt, then stir. Season the chilli to your taste, then scatter with the coriander and serve with rice or cornbread.

Notes:

1. You can store any slow cooker chili leftovers in the freezer for up to 2 months.

Slow Cooker Spaghetti Genovese

Pasta in a slow cooker? Yes! Thin shapes like spaghetti and linguine, cooked on the highest setting, work nicely. This classic Italian dish is usually made with green beans, but frozen peas work perfectly and are super convenient.

Servings: 4   **Cooking Time: 2 Hours**

Ingredients:

- 190g jar basil pesto
- 275g/9¾oz potatoes, peeled and diced into 1½-2cm/½-¼in chunks
- 300g/10½oz dried spaghetti (or linguine)
- 250g/9oz frozen peas
- 1 lemon, zested and cut in half
- salt and freshly ground black pepper

Directions:

1. Spoon about two-thirds of the pesto into the slow cooker pot. Mix in 900ml/1½ pint water and then add the potato chunks. Cover with the lid and cook on high for 2½ hours until the potatoes are tender.
2. Use a slotted spoon to lift out the majority of the potatoes. Don't worry if a few evade capture. Snap the spaghetti strands into thirds and drop into the pot. Mix well into the pesto broth, then place the potatoes on top so the pasta is submerged. Cook on high for another 30 minutes.
3. The pasta should be just about done. Stir in the frozen peas, with a splash more water if the pasta is looking dry, and cook for another 10 minutes.
4. Stir the lemon zest into the finished pasta and season with salt and pepper. Squeeze the juice from one lemon half into the pesto jar, screw on the lid and shake well to mix the juice with the remaining pesto. Spoon the spaghetti mixture onto plates and top with dollops of lemony pesto from the jar.

Notes:

1. Loosen any leftovers with a splash of water and reheat in a microwave for the best result. Any leftovers can also be frozen for up to 1 month.

Slow Cooker Bolognese

Gennaro Contaldo proves you can make an authentic bolognese in a slow cooker without any compromise on flavour. A little prep in the morning will result in a delciously rich slow cooker bolognese waiting for you when you get home.

Servings: 4 **Cooking Time: 2 Hours**

Ingredients:

- 3 tbsp olive oil
- 30g/1oz butter
- 1 onion, finely chopped
- 1 celery stalk, finely chopped
- 1 carrot, finely chopped
- 150g/5½oz pancetta, cubed
- 200g/7oz beef mince
- 200g/7oz pork mince
- 200ml/7fl oz red wine
- 1½ tbsp tomato purée
- 200ml/7fl oz beef stock
- 100ml/3½fl oz whole milk
- 400g/14oz tagliatelle, cooked according to packet instructions
- a little Parmesan, finely grated, to serve

Directions:

1. Heat the oil and butter in a large saucepan. Add the onion, celery, carrot and pancetta and cook on a gentle heat for 10 minutes, or until the onion has softened.
2. Add the mince and brown all over. Increase the heat, add the wine and cook until evaporated.
3. Dilute the tomato purée in the stock and stir into the meat. Bring to the boil then turn off the heat.
4. Transfer the mixture to a medium slow-cooker pot. Cover and cook on a low setting for 8–9 hours. Stir in the milk and cook for 30 minutes before serving. For a large slow-cooker pot, you can make double the quantity, but cooking times remain the same.
5. If cooking on the hob, instead of transferring to a slow cooker, reduce the heat to low, cover with a lid and cook on a gentle heat for 2 hours, checking and adding a little extra stock from time to time to prevent the sauce from drying out. You will need an extra 150ml/5fl oz of stock. About 10 minutes before the end of the cooking time, stir in the milk.
6. Serve the bolognese with freshly cooked tagliatelle, sprinkled with Parmesan.

Slow Cooker Black Bean Beef And Rice

This moreish beef dish uses a shortcut ready-made sauce that is made punchier with extra soy sauce and garlic. There's no time-consuming pre-browning of the beef – just throw it all in the pot in the morning and leave it to cook to a smooth, ragù-like sauce.

Servings: 4 **Cooking Time: 2 Hours**

Ingredients:

- 250g/9oz beef mince
- 170g/5¾oz sachet (or jar) black bean sauce
- 4 tsp soy sauce
- 1 onion, finely chopped
- 1 large garlic clove, crushed
- pinch chilli flakes, plus extra if spicier taste preferred (optional)
- 220g/8oz green beans, trimmed and halved
- 400g tin black beans, drained and rinsed
- 15g/½oz fresh coriander, stalks and leaves roughly chopped
- freshly ground black pepper
- 350g/12oz long-grain (or basmati) rice, cooked, to serve

Directions:

1. Roughly chop the beef mince and place in the slow cooker pot. Pour over the black bean sauce and soy sauce and use a wooden spoon to vigorously mix the beef into the sauce until it is fairly smooth with no big lumps.
2. Stir in the onion and garlic and season with plenty of black pepper. Pour in 150ml/5fl oz water and add the chilli flakes, if using. Cover with the lid and cook on low for 4 hours.
3. Stir in the green and black beans and cook for another 2–2½ hours until the green beans are soft and tender. Stir in most of the coriander.
4. Serve the beef and beans mixture over the rice and garnish with the remaining coriander.

Notes:

1. Any leftovers can be frozen for up to 3 months.

Slow Cooker Beef Stroganoff

After browning the meat, this beef stroganoff can be left to tenderise in the slow cooker throughout the day ready for dinner time. Serve with rice or tagliatelle.
You can brown the meat the night before to make things easier in the morning.

Servings: 4   **Cooking Time: 2 Hours**

Ingredients:

- 2 tbsp sunflower oil
- 600g/1lb 5oz stewing or casserole steak, cut into chunky strips
- 3 tbsp plain flour
- 2 onions, sliced
- 3 garlic cloves, crushed
- 2 beef stock cubes, crumbled
- 1 tbsp Dijon mustard
- 1 tbsp Worcestershire sauce
- 25g/1oz butter
- 200g/7oz mushrooms, sliced
- 125ml/4fl oz soured cream
- handful flatleaf or curly parsley, roughly chopped (optional)
- salt and freshly ground black pepper
- freshly cooked rice or tagliatelle, to serve

Directions:

1. Brown the steak. (You can do this the night before or in the morning, if necessary). Heat 1 tablespoon of the oil in a large frying pan over a medium–high heat and fry the meat in two batches, using the remaining oil to fry the second batch. When the chunks are sealed and browned all over, place in a bowl and sprinkle over the flour. Stir through until the dustiness has disappeared. (If your slow cooker has a browning function, you can do this step in the slow cooker.)

2. Pour 200ml/7fl oz water into the frying pan and bring to a fierce simmer, using a wooden spoon to scrape up all the meaty bits that are stuck to the bottom until the pan feels clean. Tip the meaty juices into a jug. Continue with the recipe if making straightaway or cool and then refrigerate the browned steak and jug of juices overnight if making the next day.

3. Turn the slow cooker to the high setting. Layer in the onion, garlic and steak, adding any remaining flour or juices from the bowl. Add the stock cubes, mustard and Worcestershire sauce and season with some black pepper. Top up the reserved jug of meaty juices to 650ml/20fl oz using just boiled water. Pour all over the steak mixture, add the lid and cook on low for 7–8 hours until the meat is tender.

4. Heat the butter in a frying pan over a high heat and fry the mushrooms until softened and golden. Stir into the stroganoff with the soured cream, turn the slow cooker to high and cook for another 15–25 minutes. Season with salt and pepper then stir through the parsley, if using, reserving a little to scatter over the top.

5. Garnish the stroganoff with the reserved parsley and serve with rice or tagliatelle.

Slow Cooker Moussaka

This family favourite has all of the flavour but none of the faff of the original. Instead of layering up the classic ingredients, new potatoes and aubergine chunks are cooked in a rich lamb ragu before being topped with béchamel sauce and quickly grilled to finish.

Servings: 4   **Cooking Time:** 2 Hours

Ingredients:

- 2 tsp vegetable oil, plus 2 tbsp for frying the aubergine
- 400g/14oz lamb mince
- 1 onion, finely chopped
- 3 garlic cloves, crushed
- 1 tbsp dried oregano
- 1 tsp ground cinnamon
- 2 fresh or dried bay leaves (optional)
- 690g jar passata
- 1 tsp sugar
- 1 large, or 2 small aubergines, cut into 1½–2cm/½–¾in cubes
- 350g/12oz small or baby new potatoes
- salt and freshly ground black pepper
- For the topping
- 40g/1½oz butter
- 40g/1½oz plain flour
- 400ml/14fl oz milk
- 50g/1¾oz Parmesan (or extra mature cheddar), finely grated
- 1 free-range egg

Directions:

1. Turn the slow cooker to the High setting to heat up.
2. Heat 2 teaspoons vegetable oil in a frying pan and fry the lamb, breaking it up with a wooden spoon, until brown. If preferred, tip the mince into a sieve to drain away any excess fat. Reduce the slow cooker to Low. Place the mince in the slow cooker. Add the onion, garlic, oregano, cinnamon, bay leaves, if using, passata and 250ml/9fl oz water. Season with a little salt and pepper and add the sugar. Cook for 2½–3 hours on Low.
3. Meanwhile, wipe out the lamb pan and heat 1 tablespoon vegetable oil in the pan. Cook the aubergine cubes in two batches, using the remaining tablespoon of oil for the second batch, over a very high heat until browned. Set aside.
4. Stir the aubergine and potatoes into the mixture in the slow cooker and cook for another 3 hours on Low until the potatoes are tender. Stir halfway through cooking.
5. Meanwhile, to make the topping, melt the butter and flour together in a saucepan for 2 minutes. Gradually stir in the milk to make a smooth sauce and cook over a medium heat, stirring, until the sauce starts to bubble. Take off the heat and stir in the grated cheese. Season with salt and pepper, set aside for 2 minutes, then beat in the egg.
6. Transfer the lamb mixture to a shallow baking dish and preheat the grill. Season the lamb with salt and pepper and, if the sauce has thickened too much, stir in 100ml/3½fl oz water to loosen. Spoon the béchamel sauce over the top and grill until browning.

Notes:

1. This is an ideal dish to make ahead. Just assemble in the baking dish and chill for up to 24 hours, or freeze for up to 2 months. Instead of grilling, bake in an oven, preheated to 200C/180C Fan/Gas 6, for about 30–35 minutes until the lamb sauce is bubbling around the edges and the top is browning.

Slow Cooker Vegetable Soup

A simple and versatile slow cooker vegetable soup that's perfect for an easy lunch or supper. Any leftovers will keep very well in the fridge for a couple of days, or can be frozen.

Servings: 4   Cooking Time: 2 Hours

Ingredients:

- 2 tbsp sunflower oil
- 2 onions, finely chopped
- 1 celery stick, cut into roughly 1cm/½in slices
- 2–3 carrots (around 250g/9oz), peeled and cut into roughly 1cm/½in chunks
- ½ small swede (around 275g/9¾oz), peeled and cut into roughly 1cm/½in chunks
- 3 potatoes (around 375g/13oz), peeled and cut into roughly 15mm/¾in chunks
- 1 tsp mixed dried herbs
- 600ml/20fl oz hot vegetable stock, made with 2 vegetable stock cubes
- 1/8 tsp ground turmeric (optional)
- 100ml/3½fl oz milk or water
- salt and freshly ground black pepper
- chopped fresh flatleaf parsley, to serve (optional)

Directions:

1. Heat the oil in a large non-stick frying pan and fry the onion, celery and carrots for 4–5 minutes, stirring regularly until beginning to soften. Tip into a slow cooker and add the swede, potatoes, mixed herbs, stock and turmeric, if using. Season with lots of pepper and stir well.
2. Cover and cook on High for 3½–4 hours or Low for 5–7 hours, until the vegetables are just tender.
3. Take 3 ladlefuls of the cooked soup (around 450g/1lb) and transfer to a large bowl or jug. Using a stick blender, blitz to a purée then return to the slow cooker pot and mix thoroughly to thicken the soup.
4. Stir in enough milk or water to reach the preferred consistency then cover and cook on High for a further 10–15 minutes, or until hot. Season with salt and pepper and scatter over the parsley, if using. Serve with warm crusty bread, if you like.

Notes:

1. Add a couple of diced parsnips or extra carrots instead of the swede, if you like.
2. A spoonful of curry paste will add some extra spiced flavour.
3. If you don't have a stick blender, use a food processor to blitz the vegetables and milk together before returning to the slow cooker.
4. For an extra colourful soup, add 100g/3½oz frozen peas (thawed) to the soup at the same time as the milk. You can also add any other chopped cooked vegetables at this point.
5. To stretch the soup to serve 6, add a can of drained beans at the same time as the milk.
6. If the soup cooks a little too long and the vegetables soften too much, simply blitz the whole soup until smooth and serve topped with a drizzle of cream and a sprinkling of fresh herbs.
7. You will need a slow cooker that holds at least 4 litres/7 pints for this recipe.

Slow Cooker Sesame And Miso Ribs

These sweet and sticky sesame and miso ribs are cooked to melting tenderness in the slow cooker before being caramelised with a blast of intense heat; a barbecue will give them a hint of smoky flavour, or you can brown them under a very hot grill.

Servings: 4   Cooking Time: 2 Hours

Ingredients:

- 2 racks pork ribs, about 600g/1lb 5oz each
- large piece fresh root ginger, peeled and grated
- 3 large garlic cloves, crushed
- 6 spring onions, white and green parts separated, finely sliced
- 1 red chilli, finely sliced
- 4 tbsp dark soy sauce
- 3 tbsp miso paste
- 2 tbsp toasted sesame oil
- 2 tbsp runny honey
- 1 tbsp toasted sesame seeds
- salt

Directions:

1. Preheat the slow cooker to low. Slice each rib rack in half and set aside.
2. In a large bowl, combine the ginger, garlic, spring onion whites, half the chilli, the soy sauce, miso paste and sesame oil. Add a good pinch of salt and mix well.
3. Turn each half rack of ribs in the marinade to coat, then place in the slow cooker, stacking them side by side so that they are all touching the base. Pour the marinade over the ribs and put the lid on. Cook for 6 hours until very tender.
4. Use tongs to remove the racks from the slow cooker to a plate – try not to break them up.
5. Light the barbecue about 30 minutes before you plan to start cooking (if using, you can skip this step and use the grill instead).
6. Once the slow cooker bowl is cool enough to pick up safely, strain the marinade through a sieve into a saucepan. Place over a medium heat and cook vigorously for about 5 minutes, or until the liquid has thickened to a sticky glaze. Add the honey and cook for a couple more minutes until it is well incorporated.
7. If you are not using a barbecue, preheat the grill to high.
8. Put the rib racks on a tray lined with kitchen foil and brush them liberally on both sides with the glaze, reserving a little. Place the tray of ribs on the barbecue or under the grill and cook until browned and crisped at the edges.
9. Finish by brushing with the reserved glaze. To serve, sprinkle with the reserved chilli and spring onions and the toasted sesame seeds.

Notes:

1. You could turn the racks over halfway through cooking in the slow cooker, so both sides have some time cooking in the marinade, but this is not essential.

Slow Cooker Roast Chicken

Cooking a whole chicken in a slow cooker keeps it tender and moist. Serve with all the trimmings for an easy Sunday lunch.

Each serving provides 355 kcal, 57g protein, 3g carbohydrate (of which 2g sugars), 12.5g fat (of which 3g saturates), 0.8g fibre and 1.7g salt.

Servings: 4 Cooking Time: 2 Hours

Ingredients:

- 1 onion thickly sliced
- 1.5–1.6kg/3lb 5oz–3lb 8oz whole chicken
- 1 tbsp olive or sunflower oil
- 1 tsp paprika
- 1 tsp flaked sea salt or ½ tsp fine salt
- ½ tsp coarsely ground black pepper
- freshly ground black pepper

Directions:

1. Scatter the onion over the base of a slow cooker. Remove any trussing string from the chicken and place, breast-side up, on top.
2. Pour the oil into a small bowl. Stir in the paprika, salt and pepper. Brush the oil over the chicken.
3. Cover the slow cooker with the lid and cook on high for 4–4 ½ hours or until the chicken is tender and thoroughly cooked – the meat should be almost falling off the bones. Remove the lid and pierce the thickest part of the bird with a skewer and make sure the juices run clear. If you wiggle one of the legs, it should move very easily.
4. Transfer the chicken carefully to a board to rest.
5. Strain the cooking liquor through a sieve and use as a thin gravy. (You can thicken it by simmering in a saucepan or adding a couple of teaspoons of gravy granules, if you like.)
6. Carve into slices and serve.

Notes:

1. The meat from this slow cooker roast chicken is wonderfully moist and tender so any leftovers will be great to use in sandwiches.

Slow Cooker Paprika Chicken

Chicken paprika is lightly spiced stew with tender chicken thighs, made super easy in the slow cooker. The colourful peppers and rich tomato and paprika sauce make it bright and warming. It freezes well too. Serve with rice, pasta or mashed potatoes, topped with lots of soured cream, crème fraîche or yoghurt.

Servings: 5-6   Cooking Time: 2 Hours

Ingredients:

- 2 tbsp sunflower or olive oil
- 2 onions, thinly sliced
- 2 garlic cloves, crushed
- 2–3 tsp hot smoked paprika, to taste
- 1 tbsp plain flour
- 2 x 400g tins chopped tomatoes
- 3 tbsp tomato purée
- 50ml/2fl oz chicken stock, made with 1 chicken stock cube
- 1 tsp dried mixed herbs
- 1kg/2lb 4oz chicken thigh fillets (around 12 thighs), boneless and skin removed
- 1 each large red, yellow and green pepper, seeds removed and cut into roughly 3–4cm/1¼–1½in chunks
- salt and freshly ground black pepper
- soured cream, half-fat crème fraîche or full-fat Greek-style yoghurt, to serve
- chopped fresh flatleaf parsley, to serve (optional)

Directions:

1. Heat the oil in a large non-stick frying pan and fry the onions over a medium–high heat for 5 minutes, or until softened and lightly coloured, stirring regularly. Stir in the garlic and paprika and cook for a few seconds more, stirring constantly. Tip into the pot of a slow cooker, sprinkle over the flour and toss to thoroughly coat.
2. Add the tomatoes, tomato purée, stock and mixed herbs to the slow cooker pot. Season well with a little salt and lots of ground black pepper and stir well.
3. Keeping each fillet in a neat shape, add to the slow cooker pot, nestling well into the sauce and leaving a little room between each one if possible. Don't stir again at this point as you want the thighs to retain their shape once cooked. Scatter the pepper chunks on top of the chicken and sauce but do not stir.
4. Cover with the lid and cook on High for 4–5 hours or Low for 6–8 hours, until the chicken is tender.
5. Top with generous spoonfuls of soured cream, crème fraîche or Greek-style yoghurt and scatter the parsley on top, if you like. Serve with mashed potatoes, rice or buttered pasta.

Notes:

1. Use any colour of pepper you like for this spicy stew, but a mixture looks great.
2. You will need a slow cooker that holds around 4 litres/7 pints for this recipe.
3. This stew freezes well but if you are making ahead, stick to the shorter cook time as freezing will further soften the ingredients. Thaw fully before reheating thoroughly in a microwave for the best results.

Slow Cooker Chicken Soup

A very easy classic chicken soup that freezes beautifully, this flavoursome recipe is packed with tender chicken and will go down well with all the family. Don't skip frying the onions briefly at the beginning as they make the soup extra rich and delicious.

Servings: 5-6   **Cooking Time:** 2 Hours

Ingredients:

- 2 tbsp sunflower or vegetable oil
- 2 onions, finely chopped
- 2 garlic cloves, crushed
- 65g/2¼oz plain flour
- 1.25 litres/2 pints hot chicken stock, made with 2 chicken stock cubes
- 1 tsp dried mixed herbs
- ¼ tsp ground turmeric (optional)
- 4 chicken thigh fillets, boneless and skin removed (see Tip)
- 5 tbsp milk or single cream
- salt and freshly ground black pepper
- chopped fresh flatleaf parsley or chives, to serve

Directions:

1. Heat the oil in a large non-stick frying pan and fry the onions over a medium–high heat for 3–4 minutes, or until softened, stirring constantly. Add the garlic and cook for a few seconds more, stirring.
2. Tip the onions and garlic into a slow cooker and toss with the flour. Stir in the stock, mixed herbs, turmeric, if using, and lots of freshly ground black pepper until well combined. Add the chicken to the slow cooker pot (there's no need to cut it up), cover and cook on High for 3–4 hours or Low for 5–7 hours, until the chicken is very tender.
3. Remove the lid and shred the chicken into small pieces using two forks. Stir in the milk and season with salt and pepper. Cover and cook on High for 15 minutes more, or until the soup is hot. Sprinkle over the herbs and serve with the warm crusty bread, if you like.

Notes:

1. This soup freezes beautifully, but will keep well in the fridge for a couple of days too. To freeze, leave to cool and then transfer to sealed containers. It's perfect for taking to work: thaw overnight in the fridge then reheat in the microwave or in a saucepan over a low heat.
2. You can use chicken drumsticks, skin-on thighs or legs instead of the thigh fillets if you like, adding an extra 30 minutes or so to the cooking time depending on size. Transfer to a board and remove the skin and bones after cooking. Then shred the meat and return to the pan.
3. For a thicker soup, add 2–3 tablespoons cornflour mixed with a little water at the same time as the milk or cream.
4. You will need a slow cooker that holds at least 4 litres/7 pints for this recipe.

Slow-Cooked Tomato And Fennel Stew With Pearl Barley

Pearl barley is seriously underrated. It makes a wonderful base for a stew and pairs well with the fennel and cannellini beans. This dish makes a lovely and light dinner.

Each serving provides 496 kcal, 16g protein, 58g carbohydrates (of which 9g sugars), 18.5g fat (of which 2.5g saturates), 16g fibre and 2.5g salt.

Servings: 4   Cooking Time: 30 Mins.-1 Hour

Ingredients:

- 150g/5½oz pearl barley, rinsed
- 400ml/14fl oz vegetable stock
- 2 x 400g tins cannellini beans, drained and rinsed
- 600g/1lb 5oz fennel, finely chopped
- 100g/3½oz black olives, stones removed, roughly chopped
- 2 garlic cloves, crushed
- 2 bay leaves
- ½ tbsp olive oil
- 8 large tomatoes on the vine
- For the basil and pine nut dressing
- 30g/1oz fresh basil, very finely chopped
- 2½ tbsp olive oil
- ½ tbsp lemon juice, plus extra if needed
- 15g/½oz pine nuts, roughly chopped
- sea salt and freshly ground black pepper

Directions:

1. Preheat the oven to 200C/180C Fan/Gas 6.
2. Place the pearl barley, stock, cannellini beans, fennel, olives, garlic, bay leaves and oil in a casserole dish or small, deep roasting tin and stir to combine. Place the tomatoes on top, cover tightly with kitchen foil or a lid and cook for 1 hour.
3. Meanwhile, to make the basil and pine nut dressing, mix together the basil, oil, pinch sea salt, lemon juice and pine nuts in a small bowl. Set aside.
4. Leave the stew to stand for 10 minutes. Carefully lift the tomatoes on to a separate plate then stir through half of the dressing into the stew. Taste and add more salt, pepper and lemon juice, if needed. Return the tomatoes to the dish.
5. Drizzle over the remaining dressing and serve immediately.

Slow Cooker Creamy Chicken, Lemon And Basil Pasta

Pasta works well in this slow-cooked creamy chicken dish: the pasta soaks up all the lovely, summery flavours as everything gently bubbles away.

Servings: 4 **Cooking Time: 1-2 Hours**

Ingredients:

- 1 chicken stock pot or cube
- 675ml/24fl oz boiling water
- 1–2 tbsp olive oil
- 500g/1lb 2oz boneless, skinless chicken thighs, cut into bite-sized pieces
- 300g/10½oz spirali pasta
- 2 large courgettes, cut into large dice
- 2 garlic cloves, finely chopped
- 1 small lemon, finely grated zest
- 25g/1oz pack of basil, roughly chopped, plus extra small leaves to serve
- 170g/6oz full-fat crème fraîche
- salt and freshly ground black pepper

Directions:

1. Preheat the slow cooker to high. Put the chicken stock cube in a measuring jug and add the boiling water. Stir to dissolve the stock.
2. Heat 1 tablespoon of the olive oil in a large non-stick frying pan over a high heat. Add half the chicken and cook until it is browned all over.
3. Transfer the chicken to the slow cooker pot with a slotted spoon, leaving the fat in the pan. Cook the remaining chicken in the same way and add to the slow cooker, then add the pasta to the slow cooker.
4. If needed, add more olive oil to the pan, then add the courgettes and cook over a high heat for a couple of minutes until browned. Remove them to a plate.
5. Reduce the heat below the frying pan and add the garlic. Cook for a few seconds to take off the raw tang. Pour in a little of the stock and stir with a wooden spoon to loosen any bits of chicken that are stuck to the bottom. Tip it into the slow cooker, along with the remaining stock. Add the lemon zest and basil and season with salt and pepper, then give everything a good stir.
6. Spread the courgettes over the top of the mixture, cover with the lid and cook for 1 hour.
7. Add the crème fraîche and give everything a good stir. Turn the heat off, replace the lid and leave to rest for 15 minutes.
8. Give it another stir, then taste and adjust the seasoning. Serve scattered with a few fresh basil leaves.

Notes:

1. This recipe was tested in a medium-sized cooker with a ceramic bowl; if your slow cooker has a metal bowl insert, it may cook more quickly and not need the resting time.

Slow-Cooked Roast Chicken With Gravy

Use up any leftover chicken in sandwiches or in a quick chicken curry, leftover chicken will keep in the fridge for 1 day.

Servings: 4   Cooking Time: 2 Hours

Ingredients:

- For the roast chicken
- 2 carrots, cut into chunks
- 2 celery stalks, trimmed, cut into chunks
- 1 onion, cut into six
- 1 x 2kg/4½lb whole chicken
- ½ lemon, cut into quarters
- small bunch fresh mixed herbs (sage, thyme and rosemary)
- dash vegetable oil
- salt and freshly ground black pepper
- potatoes and roasted vegetables, to serve
- For the gravy
- 275ml/½ pint chicken stock
- 30g/1¼oz butter
- 1 tbsp plain flour

Directions:

1. Preheat the oven to 140C/120C Fan/Gas 1.
2. Put the carrots, celery and onion in a roasting tray and place the chicken on top. Stuff the cavity of the chicken with the lemon and herbs, then drizzle with the oil, rubbing it into the skin. Season, to taste, with salt and pepper.
3. Roast the chicken for 3 hours, basting the skin with the juices halfway through. Increase the oven temperature to its highest setting and continue to roast the chicken for 5-10 minutes to crisp up the skin. Remove it from the roasting tray and check it is cooked through (see tips), then set aside on a platter to rest for 10-15 minutes. Reserve the vegetables and cooking juices in the roasting tray.
4. Meanwhile, for the gravy, strain the reserved vegetables and cooking juices through a fine sieve into a saucepan, squeezing the vegetables with the back of a wooden spoon to extract maximum flavour. Add the stock to the pan and bring to the boil.
5. Put the roasting tray over a low heat and add the butter. As the butter melts, scrape up any burned bits from the bottom of the tray using a wooden spoon. Whisk in the flour until it forms a paste.
6. Gradually pour the hot roasting juices and stock back into the roasting tray, whisking after each addition, until all the liquid is incorporated and the gravy has thickened. Season with a little salt. Heat until just bubbling, then continue to cook the gravy, stirring well, for 5 minutes. Season with a pinch of salt.
7. Strain the gravy through a sieve into a serving jug. Keep warm. Just before serving, stir any juices released by the rested chicken in to the gravy.
8. To serve, carve the roast chicken at the table and serve with roasted vegetables and potatoes. Drizzle with the gravy.

Notes:

1. Tip 1: Buy the best-quality chicken you can afford - you'll really taste the difference!
2. Tip 2: To check the chicken is cooked through, insert a skewer into the thickest part of the thigh; if the juices run clear and no trace of pink remains, the chicken is ready. If there is any sign of pink, return it to the oven until cooked through.
3. Tip 3: Resting the meat is very important to ensure it is served at its most tender and juicy. Do not cover it as it rests, because this will cause the skin to turn from crisp to soggy.

Slow Cooker Chocolate Self-Saucing Pudding

This clever chocolate pudding recipe uses a slow cooker as opposed to an oven to save energy. The rich, decadent results are easy to achieve, as the slow cooker does most of the work.

Servings: 6-8   **Cooking Time: 2 Hours**

Ingredients:

- 170g/5¾oz unsalted butter, diced, plus extra for greasing
- 170g/5¾oz dark chocolate (minimum 70% cocoa solids), roughly chopped
- 300g/10½oz golden caster sugar
- 3 free-range eggs
- 90g/3¼oz plain flour
- 65g/2¼oz cocoa powder
- 150g/5½oz light brown sugar

Directions:

1. Lightly grease the bowl of a slow cooker (we used one that had a 3.5 litre/6 pint capacity). Melt the butter and chocolate in a large saucepan, stir together and whisk in the sugar and eggs. Fold in the flour and 40g/1½oz cocoa powder until just combined, then spoon into the prepared slow cooker bowl.
2. Mix the remaining cocoa powder with the light brown sugar in a heatproof bowl or jug. Whisk in 180ml/6¼fl oz boiling water until well combined. Carefully pour the liquid over the top of the mixture in the slow cooker.
3. Lay a clean tea towel over the top of the bowl and use the lid to clamp it in place (do not let the tea towel touch the mixture below).
4. Cook on low for 2¼ hours, then remove the lid and tea towel for 15–20 minutes, cooking until the sauce is bubbling around the sides and the top of the sponge is firm. Serve immediately. Alternatively, if preferred, leave the pudding to cool before serving, as the gooey centre will set like a brownie.

Veggie Bean Stew

A simple stew that tastes delicious. Perfect for rainy days when you don't want to go shopping!

Servings: 2   Cooking Time: 30 Mins.-1 Hour

Ingredients:

- 1 tbsp olive oil
- 1 small onion, finely chopped
- 1 stick celery, finely chopped
- 1 garlic clove, crushed
- 1 small sweet potato, cut into 1cm/½in dice
- 400g tin chopped tomatoes
- 1 tsp tomato purée
- 1 tsp dried oregano
- 1 tsp smoked paprika
- pinch dried chilli flakes
- 200ml/7fl oz vegetable stock (made from ½ stock cube or ½ tsp bouillon powder)
- 400g tin butter beans, drained and rinsed
- handful kale, spinach or other leafy green vegetable
- salt and freshly ground black pepper

Directions:

1. Heat the oil in a lidded saucepan over a medium heat. Add the onion and celery and sweat for 5 minutes with the lid on.
2. Add the garlic and sweet potato and cook for a further 5 minutes, until beginning to soften.
3. Add the chopped tomatoes, tomato purée, oregano, paprika, chilli flakes and stock. Stir well and bring to the boil. Reduce the heat and simmer with the lid on for 10 minutes.
4. Add the butterbeans and simmer without the lid on for 10–15 minutes, or until the sweet potato is soft.
5. Add the kale and allow to wilt for 2 minutes. Stir well, check the seasoning and serve.

Notes:

1. Use any beans or leftover veg you have for this recipe.

Vegetable Casserole With Dumplings

This wholesome warming one-pot vegetarian casserole is perfect for cold January nights. It's full of beans, celeriac and topped with fluffy dumplings. This wholesome one pot is perfect for cold nights – simple enough to whip up quickly, but smart enough to serve to friends.

Servings: 4   **Cooking Time: 30 Mins.-1 Hour**

Ingredients:

- For the stew
- 1 onion, chopped
- 1 tbsp olive oil
- 2 tbsp butter
- 25g/1oz plain flour
- 1 tsp English mustard powder
- 150ml/5fl oz apple juice
- 900ml/1½ pint vegetable stock
- 2 tbsp wholegrain mustard
- 4 bay leaves
- 450g/1lb peeled celeriac, chopped into 1–2cm/½–¾in thick, small wedges
- 2 leeks, trimmed and cut into 2cm/¾in chunks
- 100g/3½oz baby spinach
- 400g tin cannellini beans, drained and rinsed
- 1 tbsp chopped fresh tarragon
- salt and freshly ground black pepper
- For the dumplings
- 150g/5½oz self-raising flour, plus extra for rolling
- ½ tsp baking powder
- 25g/1oz cold butter, diced
- 2 tbsp chopped fresh tarragon, plus a little extra to serve if preferred
- ¼ tsp salt
- 75g/2¾ oz natural yoghurt

Directions:

1. Put the onion, olive oil and butter In an ovenproof, wide casserole dish. Fry over a low heat until the onion is soft and beginning to turn golden brown. Stir in the flour and mustard powder and cook, stirring, for 2 minutes. Gradually stir in the apple juice, followed by the stock, then the wholegrain mustard and bay leaves. Bring the sauce to a simmer.
2. Add the celeriac and leek and continue simmering for 15 minutes, or until the vegetables are almost tender. Take off the heat and remove the bay leaves. Stir in the spinach, followed by the beans and tarragon. Season to taste. Preheat the oven to 200C/180C Fan/Gas 6.
3. For the dumplings, mix the flour and baking powder in a mixing bowl. Rub in the diced butter until you can only feel small lumps, then stir in the tarragon and salt. Mix the yogurt with 2 tablespoons of cold water, then drizzle over the flour and mix quickly to form a sticky dough. Flour your hands, then quickly roll into 12 balls.
4. Arrange the dumplings on top of the bean stew. Cover the casserole with the lid and bake in the oven for 10 minutes. Remove the lid and bake for 15–18 minutes more, or until the dumplings are puffed up and just turning golden brown on top. Spoon into shallow bowls to serve, scattered with extra tarragon if you like.

Gingerbread With Salted Caramel And Clotted Cream

Curl up on the sofa with a cuppa and this gingerbread cake drizzled with a salted caramel sauce. The perfect treat for cosy nights in.

Servings: 4   Cooking Time: 10-30 Mins.

Ingredients:

- For the gingerbread cake
- 140g/5oz self-raising flour
- pinch sea salt flakes
- 100g/3½oz golden syrup
- 100g/3½oz dark brown soft sugar
- 70g/2½oz butter, plus extra for greasing
- 1 free-range egg
- 40g/1½oz stem ginger, puréed or very finely chopped
- 6 tbsp full-fat milk
- For the salted caramel
- 120g/4½oz caster sugar
- 120g/4½oz cream
- 20g/½oz butter
- To serve
- clotted cream
- homemade pickled pear (optional)

Directions:

1. Preheat the oven to 170C/150C Fan/Gas 3½. Grease a 18cm/7in square cake tin. Dampen a piece of baking parchment, scrunch it up until flexible and line the tin.
2. In a large bowl, mix the flour and salt then set aside.
3. Put the syrup, sugar and butter into a heatproof bowl. Bring a pan of water to a simmer and place the bowl on top. Heat until incorporated, stirring continuously.
4. Meanwhile, in a jug, beat together the egg, ginger and milk. Remove the syrup mixture from the heat and gently whisk in the milk mixture until combined. Pour the wet ingredients into the bowl containing the flour and fold together. Once evenly combined, pour the batter into the cake tin and sprinkle with more salt.
5. Bake for 20–25 minutes until a skewer comes out clean and the top bounces back when pressed. Leave to cool in the tin.
6. For the salted caramel, put a high-sided saucepan over a medium heat. Add the sugar and 20ml/½fl oz of water and heat for 5–7 minutes, swirling the pan occasionally until a dark caramel forms. Do not stir and take care: boiling sugar is extremely hot. Immediately add the butter, swirling it into the caramel. Slowly stir in the cream until incorporated. Add a pinch of salt.
7. Cut the cake into four and drizzle with the salted caramel. Serve with a large spoonful of clotted cream, and pickled pears if using.

Chipotle Pinto Bean Stew

Try this smoky chipotle bean stew for a satisfying veggie dinner. You can make this in half an hour using tinned beans but dried beans do come out a bit cheaper.

Each serving provides 404 kcal, 18g protein, 51g carbohydrate (of which 12g sugars), 13g fat (of which 5.5g saturates), 4g fibre and 1.1g salt.

Servings: 4   Cooking Time: 30 Mins.-1 Hour

Ingredients:

- 250g/9oz dried pinto beans or 2 x 400g tins pinto beans, drained
- olive oil, for frying
- 2 onions, finely chopped
- 2 celery sticks, finely chopped
- 3 garlic cloves, crushed or grated
- 2 tsp ground cumin
- ½ tsp ground cinnamon
- 1 tbsp chipotle paste (approx. 20g/¾oz)
- 30g/1oz tomato purée
- 400g tin chopped tomatoes
- 1 vegetable stock cube
- 200g/7oz frozen sweetcorn (or tinned sweetcorn, drained)
- salt and freshly ground black pepper
- To serve
- 50g/1¾oz pickled jalapeño chillies, drained (optional)
- 150ml/5fl oz soured cream or yoghurt (plant-based, if you prefer)
- pinch smoked paprika (optional)
- wholemeal flour tortilla wraps, made into chips (optional)

Directions:

1. If you're using dried pinto beans, tip them into a large bowl or saucepan, cover with cold water and leave to soak overnight. Drain the beans in a colander, rinse thoroughly, then tip into a pan and cover with plenty of fresh cold water. Set over a high heat, bring to the boil, then reduce the heat and simmer gently for 1 hour, or until soft. Drain and set aside to cool.
2. Heat a splash of olive oil in a casserole or large saucepan and fry the onion, celery and garlic gently for 5 minutes until soft.
3. Add the cumin and cinnamon, fry for 30 seconds, then stir in the chipotle paste and tomato purée. Fry for a further minute, then add the chopped tomatoes, stock cube and pinto beans.
4. Pour in 200ml/7fl oz water, bring to the boil, then reduce the heat and simmer for 20 minutes. Stir in the sweetcorn and cook for a couple of minutes more to warm through. Season to taste.
5. Spoon the stew into warmed bowls, then top with the jalapeños, soured cream and a pinch of smoked paprika. Serve with homemade tortilla chips for dipping.

Notes:

1. If you have young children who don't like spicy food, you can substitute 1 teaspoon of smoked paprika for the chipotle paste. You can also stir the chipotle paste into adult portions right before serving. It will taste just as good.
2. Tinned beans work just as well for this dish; use whatever you have in the cupboard. If you don't have pinto, try using kidney beans or black beans.
3. When soaking dried beans overnight, it's always best to make a big batch. Once cooked and cooled they can be portioned and frozen. Freeze the beans on a baking tray and then pour them into a bag. This makes it easy to scoop out the amount you need.

Fennel And Butternut Squash Stew With Cannellini Beans

A vegan butternut squash stew for your pressure cooker that's simple, healthy and quick to cook – from chopping board to table in 30 minutes.

Each serving provides 191 kcal, 7g protein, 20g carbohydrates (of which 6g sugars), 6.5g fat (of which 1g saturates), 9g fibre and 1.3g salt.

Servings: 4 Cooking Time: 10-30 Mins.

Ingredients:

- 2 tbsp olive oil
- 1 large fennel bulb, approx. 250g/9oz, sliced, fronds reserved
- 2 garlic cloves, grated
- 1 tsp sea salt
- ½ tsp black pepper
- 2 bay leaves
- ½ tbsp fennel seeds, lightly crushed
- 4 tbsp dry white wine
- 1 butternut squash, peeled, seeds removed (approx. 425g/15oz), cut into 2cm/¾in pieces
- 400g tin cannellini beans (or butter beans), rinsed and drained
- 500ml/18fl oz vegetable stock
- 2 red chillies, 1 whole and 1 finely sliced

Directions:

1. Heat the oil in the pressure cooker over a medium heat. Add the fennel, garlic, salt and pepper and fry for 4–6 minutes, until fragrant.
2. Add the bay leaves and fennel seeds and fry for another minute. Pour in the wine and stir with a wooden spoon, scraping up any browned bits from the bottom of the pan.
3. Add the squash, beans, stock and the whole red chilli. Fix the lid on the pressure cooker and place over a high heat until it reaches pressure. Reduce the heat to medium–low and cook for 10 minutes. (If using an electric pressure cooker, use the high pressure setting for 10 minutes).
4. Remove the pressure cooker from the heat and leave to depressurise.
5. To serve, top the stew with the sliced red chilli and reserved fennel fronds. Serve with crusty bread.

Malva Pudding

A traditional Southern African pudding, this toffee-like sponge dessert is soaked in a sweet cream syrup which ups the ante in the sweetness stakes! Believe it or not, it welcomes serving with cream or a scoop of ice cream, if preferred.

Servings: 8   **Cooking Time:** 30 Mins.-1 Hour

Ingredients:

- For the pudding
- 150g/5½oz plain flour
- 1½ tsp bicarbonate of soda
- 2 tbsp apricot jam
- 2 free-range eggs
- 175g/6oz light brown sugar
- 55g/2oz caster sugar
- 200ml/7fl oz milk (preferably full-fat)
- 50g/1¾oz melted butter, plus extra for greasing
- 1 tbsp white wine or spirit vinegar
- For the sauce
- 200ml/7fl oz double cream
- 100ml/3½fl oz milk (preferably full-fat)
- 160g/5¾oz caster sugar
- 80g/2¾oz butter
- 1 tbsp vanilla extract
- cream or ice cream, to serve (optional)

Directions:

1. Preheat the oven to 180C/160C Fan/Gas 4. Grease an ovenproof ceramic or glass dish that is approximately 20x30cm/8x12in.
2. Place the flour in a large bowl and sprinkle over the bicarbonate of soda. In a separate bowl, whisk together the jam, eggs and sugars until pale in colour. Mix together the milk, butter and vinegar. Alternate adding a bit of the milk mixture and a bit of the flour to the egg mixture, until everything is combined and forms a smooth batter.
3. Pour the batter into the prepared dish, cover with kitchen foil and bake for 35–40 minutes until the sponge is cooked through and bouncy to touch. Then remove the tinfoil and return the sponge to the oven for another 10 minutes to brown the top. The edges will turn a dark brown which makes them caramel-like and chewy. (Err on the side of longer in the oven here so the sponge can absorb the sauce.)
4. To make the sauce, heat all of the ingredients and 5 tablespoons water in a saucepan over a medium heat. Simmer for 2 minutes then turn off the heat.
5. When cooked, remove the pudding from the oven and set aside for a few minutes. Pour over the hot sauce and leave to soak up for at least 10 minutes before serving. Serve the pudding with cream or ice cream, if desired.

Notes:

1. If preferred, add 2 tablespoons brandy to the sauce.
2. This can be made in advance and reheated to serve, although we suggest it's always best just out of the oven. The sponge will absorb more liquid so be sure to cover and reheat the pudding to avoid drying out. To serve leftovers, you will need to reheat the sponge as it will solidify.

Mediterranean Bean Stew With Potato Griddle Cakes

Create a taste of the Mediterranean with this hearty vegan stew served with potato cakes. The perfect everyday meal.

Each serving provides 471kcal, 13.5g protein, 51g carbohydrate (of which 13g sugars), 21g fat (of which 4g saturates), 13g fibre and 0.8g salt.

Servings: 4-6   Cooking Time: 30 Mins.-1 Hour

Ingredients:

- 2 tbsp extra-virgin olive oil, plus extra to serve
- 2 red onions cut into wedges
- 2 courgettes, chopped into 1cm/½in batons
- 150g/5½oz celeriac, cut into cubes
- 1 garlic clove, finely chopped
- 2 tbsp tomato purée
- 1 tbsp smoked paprika
- 1 x 440g/1lb tin chopped tomatoes
- 200ml/7fl oz vegetable stock
- 1 x 400g/14oz tin butter beans or mixed beans, drained
- handful fresh basil
- 1 lemon, zest only
- 100g/3½oz cooked broad beans
- For the griddled potato cakes
- 250g/9oz mashed potatoes
- 1 tsp baking powder
- 100g/3½oz plain flour
- salt and freshly ground black pepper
- 1 tbsp fresh thyme
- 2 tbsp vegetable oil

Directions:

1. For the stew, heat two tablespoons of the oil in a casserole pan and fry the onions, courgettes, celeriac and garlic for 4-5 minutes.
2. Add the tomato purée and smoked paprika and cook for a further 4-5 minutes. Add the chopped tomatoes and stock, bring to boil, then reduce to a simmer for 20-25 minutes.
3. Stir in the butter beans, basil and lemon zest and cook for a further 10 minutes, then stir in the broad beans. Finish the stew with a good glug of extra-virgin olive oil.
4. Meanwhile, for the griddled potato cakes, mix the ingredients together in a bowl until well combined, then shape the potato mixture into six patties.
5. Heat the oil in a frying pan and fry the patties for 3-4 minutes on each side, or until crisp and golden-brown on both sides.
6. To serve, ladle the stew into serving bowl and serve the potato cakes alongside.

Notes:

1. You can buy readymade mashed potato from the chiller and freezer sections of most supermarkets, which will make the potato cakes much quicker to make.

Red-Red Stew With Spiced Plantain

Traditionally a red-red stew is made with palm oil and tomatoes. We've updated this version of the common Ghanaian dish to use vegetable oil.

Servings: 4   **Cooking Time:** 1-2 Hours

Ingredients:

- For the kelewele dry spice mix
- 2 tbsp ground ginger
- 1 tbsp ground cinnamon
- 1 tbsp ground nutmeg
- 1 tbsp cayenne pepper
- ½ tbsp ground cloves
- For the stew
- 200g/7oz dried black-eyed beans or 1 x 400g tin black-eyed beans, drained and rinsed
- 75ml/2½fl oz vegetable oil
- 2 red onions, finely chopped
- 2.5cm/1in piece fresh root ginger, finely grated
- ½ tbsp dried chilli flakes
- ½ red scotch bonnet chilli, deseeded and diced
- ½ tsp curry powder
- ½ tbsp chilli powder
- 1 x 400g tin chopped tomatoes
- 4 plum tomatoes, roughly chopped
- 1 tbsp tomato purée
- 1 tsp sea salt
- ½ tsp ground black pepper
- garri, for garnish
- For the spiced plantain
- 1 heaped tbsp kelewele dry spice mix, from above
- 1 small red onion, grated
- 5cm/2in fresh root ginger, grated
- pinch sea salt
- vegetable oil, for deep-frying
- 4-6 ripe plantains, peeled and cut into chips
- handful roasted peanuts, crushed
- To serve
- handful micro coriander cress
- 1 red chilli, thinly sliced
- handful nasturtium flowers and leaves

Directions:

1. Mix the ingredients for the kelewele dry spice mix together in a lidded jar and set aside.
2. If using dried beans, rinse and place in a large saucepan, cover with water and bring to the boil, then simmer for at least 1 hour until the beans are tender.
3. Heat the oil in a large saucepan over a low-medium heat. Add the onion, ginger, chilli flakes and scotch bonnet and fry gently until the onion is translucent.
4. Add the curry and chilli powders and stir well. Add the tomatoes, tomato purée, salt and pepper and cook for 45–60 minutes.
5. Add the beans, reduce the heat and cook for 30 minutes, stirring occasionally, until the beans are tender and the tomatoes have lost their sharp taste.
6. For the spiced plantain, mix the dry spice mix with the onion, ginger, salt and 2 tablespoon of oil in a bowl.
7. Coat the plantain in the spice mix and leave to marinate for at least 20 minutes.
8. Preheat a deep-fat fryer to 180C. (CAUTION: hot oil can be dangerous. Do not leave unattended.) Fry the plantain chips in batches until they float to the surface and are an even golden colour. Remove with a slotted spoon and drain on kitchen paper.
9. To serve, spoon the stew into large bowls and sprinkle the garri over the top. Serve the plantain on the side, sprinkled with the crushed peanuts.

Chickpeas With Harissa And Yoghurt

Chickpeas are filling, delicious, easy to cook and cheap, making them the perfect choice for students. Each serving provides 357 kcal, 14.5g protein, 30g carbohydrates (of which 11g sugars), 18g fat (of which 3g saturates), 10g fibre and 0.4g salt.

Servings: 2   Cooking Time: 10-30 Mins.

Ingredients:

- 2 tbsp olive oil
- ½ red onion, thinly sliced
- 1 courgette, halved lengthways and sliced
- 400g tin chickpeas, drained and rinsed
- 2 tbsp harissa paste
- 8–10 cherry tomatoes, halved
- ½ lemon, juice only
- 6 tbsp plain yoghurt
- finely chopped flatleaf parsley or coriander
- salt and freshly ground black pepper

Directions:

1. Heat the oil in a frying pan and gently fry the onion and courgette for 4–5 minutes, stirring regularly, until softened and beginning to brown.
2. Add the chickpeas, harissa and tomatoes and cook for 3–4 minutes, stirring occassionally, until the tomatoes are softened but still holding their shape. Add a splash of water if the mixture begins to stick.
3. Add a squeeze of lemon juice and season with salt and pepper.
4. Spoon the yoghurt onto two plates or shallow bowls, top with the warm chickpeas and sprinkle with the herbs. Serve immediately.

Spicy Autumn Squash Stew

This easy one-pot stew is endlessly adaptable, see the variations in the tips section below.

Servings: 4   Cooking Time: 10-30 Mins.

Ingredients:

- 2 tbsp sunflower oil
- 1 onion, finely chopped
- 2 garlic cloves, finely chopped
- 1 small red chilli, very finely chopped (or dried red chilli flakes, to taste)
- 1 red pepper, cut into short strips
- 6 spring onions, sliced diagonally
- 1 tsp ground coriander
- 1 medium butternut squash, peeled, deseeded, and rough cut into 2cm/1in pieces
- 2 handfuls cherry tomatoes, halved
- 400ml tin coconut milk
- ½ lemon, juice only
- salt and freshly ground black pepper
- small bunch coriander, leaves and stalks chopped separately

Directions:

1. Heat the oil in a a heavy-bottomed saucepan, add the onion, garlic, chilli, red pepper and spring onions and cook gently for about 5 minutes until soft.
2. Add the ground coriander and cook for a minute then add the squash, coriander stalks, and tomatoes. Cook this for a further 5 minutes.
3. Add the coconut milk and simmer, partially covered, for 15 minutes or until the squash is tender.
4. Add the lemon juice, season with salt and freshly ground black pepper to taste and sprinkle over the coriander leaves. Serve with white or brown basmati rice.

Notes:

1. Substitute sweet potatoes for the squash and half a 400ml tin of chopped tomatoes for the cherry tomatoes. Or add green pepper and half a 400ml tin drained chickpeas. For extra protein, add 3–4 skinless chicken breasts, cut into chunks or 200g/7oz prawns, a handful of mangetout, and a dash of fish sauce.

Vegan Chilli

This delicious and healthy vegan chilli recipe gets its smoky flavour from chipotle paste, made from smoked jalapeno peppers. You can use any tins of beans that you like, or even tinned lentils.

This meal provides 501 kcal, 18g protein, 71g carbohydrate (of which 18g sugars), 16g fat (of which 3g saturates), 17g fibre and 1.4g salt per portion.

Servings: 4   Cooking Time: 30 Mins.-1 Hour

Ingredients:

- For the chipotle stew
- 2 tbsp olive oil
- 2 medium onions, sliced
- 1 yellow pepper, deseeded, cut into chunks
- 1 medium sweet potato (approximately 300g/10½oz), peeled, cut into chunks
- 1 tsp ground coriander
- 1 tbsp plain flour
- 400g tin chopped tomatoes
- 2 tbsp chipotle paste (available at larger supermarkets and delicatessens)
- 400g tin cannellini beans, rinsed and drained
- 400g tin red kidney beans, rinsed and drained
- salt and freshly ground black pepper
- vegan crème fraîche, to serve (optional)
- For the coriander quinoa
- 150g/5oz quinoa, rinsed
- 1 ripe but firm avocado, halved, stone removed, flesh scooped out
- 1 lime, juice only
- 4 spring onions, finely sliced
- 1½ tbsp chopped fresh coriander, plus extra to garnish
- salt and freshly ground black pepper

Directions:

1. Heat the oil in a large heavy-based saucepan over a medium heat. Add the onions and fry for 2-3 minutes, stirring well. Add the pepper and sweet potato and fry for 3-4 minutes. Sprinkle over the coriander and flour, stir to combine, continue to fry for 30-40 seconds.
2. Add the chopped tomatoes, chipotle paste, beans and 600ml/20fl oz cold water to the saucepan. Stir well to combine and season with salt and pepper.
3. Bring to the boil, then simmer for 18-20 minutes, stirring more and more regularly as the cooking time progresses, until all of the vegetables are tender. Add water if it starts to dry out.
4. Meanwhile, for the quinoa, half-fill a saucepan with water and bring to the boil. Add the quinoa, stir well, then simmer for 12-15 minutes, or until just tender.
5. Cut the avocado into chunks and drizzle over the lime juice.
6. Drain the quinoa and put in a large bowl. Set aside to cool for 3-5 minutes, then fluff with a fork. Stir in the avocado, spring onions and coriander. Season with salt and pepper and mix well.
7. Spoon the quinoa onto plates and top with a ladleful of the stew. Serve a dollop of soured cream alongside.

Notes:

1. Tip 1: This stew will work well with any canned beans.
2. Tip 2: If preferred, substitute the quinoa with 200g/7oz rice.
3. Tip 3: If you can't find chipotle paste, season the stew with 1 teaspoon of paprika and 2 tablespoons of tomato purée.

Aubergine And Black Bean Bowl

Servings: 2   Cooking Time: 30 Mins.-1 Hour

Ingredients:

- 1 aubergine, cut into 2cm/¾in cubes
- olive oil, for cooking
- 2 x 400g tins black beans, drained
- 30g/1oz tomato purée
- 1 tbsp red wine vinegar
- 1 tsp ground cumin
- 1 tsp smoked paprika
- pinch sugar
- salt and freshly ground black pepper
- For the tortilla chips
- 2 wholemeal tortilla wraps, cut into triangles
- To serve
- 50g/1¾oz feta, crumbled
- 15g/½oz fresh coriander, roughly chopped
- quick pickled onions (optional)
- 1 lime, cut into wedges

Directions:

1. Preheat the oven to 220C/200C Fan/Gas 7 and put a roasting tin on the middle shelf to heat up.
2. Put the cubed aubergine in the heated roasting tin and drizzle with the olive oil. Season with salt and pepper, mix well and roast for 20 minutes until softened and crisp at the edges.
3. To make the tortilla chips, brush the tortilla triangles with a little oil and season with a pinch of salt. Arrange them on a baking tray in a single layer. Bake for 6–7 minutes until crisp, keeping an eye on them as they can burn easily. Set aside.
4. Mix the beans, tomato purée, vinegar, spices and sugar together in a bowl, then roughly crush with a potato masher. Stir in 200ml/7fl oz warm water, then add to the roasting tin with the aubergines and return to the oven for 5 minutes.
5. Spoon the aubergine mixture into 2 bowls and top with the feta, coriander, pickled onions and lime wedges. Serve with the homemade tortilla chips for dipping.

Ultimate Vegan Stew

A deliciously warming one-pot winter dish that uses meaty-textured jackfruit for the ultimate vegan stew. Each serving provides 485 kcal, 6.5g protein, 56g carbohydrates (of which 11g sugars), 19g fat (of which 4g saturates), 9g fibre and 2.4g salt.

Servings: 4   Cooking Time: 1-2 Hours

Ingredients:

- 4 tbsp vegan margarine
- 2 x 540g tins (or 3 x 400g tins) jackfruit in brine, drained and rinsed
- 2 tbsp soy sauce
- 1 brown onion, chopped
- 2 celery sticks, finely chopped
- 4 garlic cloves, finely chopped
- 2 tbsp plain flour
- 250ml/9fl oz vegan-friendly red wine
- 4 sprigs fresh thyme, leaves picked
- 4 carrots, cut into 1cm/½in slices
- 750g/1lb 10oz potatoes, peeled and cut into bite-size chunks
- 2 bay leaves
- 500ml/18fl oz vegetable stock
- 250ml/9fl oz hot water
- salt and pepper

Directions:

1. Put 3 tablespoons of the margarine in a large lidded saucepan over a medium heat. Add the jackfruit and a small pinch of salt and pepper. Fry for 15–20 minutes, or until golden brown, adding more margarine if necessary.
2. Once the jackfruit is golden brown, remove from the heat and stir in 1 tablespoon of soy sauce, then tip the jackfruit into a bowl and wipe out the pan.
3. Put the pan back over a medium heat and add the remaining 1 tablespoon of margarine. Add the onion and celery and fry for 8 minutes. Add the garlic and fry for 1 minute, then stir in the flour.
4. Pour in the wine and simmer for 2 minutes. Add the thyme, carrots, potatoes, bay, stock, hot water and the remaining tablespoon of soy sauce. Bring to the boil, then reduce the heat, put the lid on and simmer for 40–50 minutes, or until the vegetables are tender. Stir the cooked jackfruit into the stew and simmer for 1 minute before serving.

Notes:

1. In the summer, swap the carrots for French beans and/or peppers, adding them for the last 10–15 minutes of cooking time, and use new potatoes.

Greek-Style Beans

Servings: 4 Cooking Time: 10-30 Mins.

Ingredients:

- 2 tbsp olive oil
- ½ red onion, thinly sliced
- 400g tin chopped tomatoes
- 1 tbsp runny honey
- 1 small red chilli, deseeded and finely chopped
- 1 tsp ground cinnamon
- ½ tsp paprika
- 1 tsp dried oregano
- 400g tin butter beans, drained and rinsed (can also use chickpeas or other white beans)
- 150g/5½oz chard, spinach or spring greens, roughly chopped
- 10g fresh flatleaf parsley, leaves and stalks finely chopped

Directions:

1. Preheat the oven to 200C/180C Fan/Gas 6.
2. Heat the oil in a large oven-proof frying pan over a medium heat. Add the onion and season with salt and pepper. Cook for 2-3 minutes until softened.
3. Add the tomatoes, honey, chilli, cinnamon, paprika and oregano. Simmer for a few minutes. Stir in the beans and the greens.
4. Bake for 20 minutes until the edges brown. (If you don't have an ovenproof frying pan, tip the mixture into a baking dish.)
5. Scatter over the parsley and serve.

Notes:

1. Use whatever beans and greens you have, it'll taste great!

Black-Eyed Bean Stew

This healthy bean stew is quick to put together, packed with protein and easy to assemble from storecupboard ingredients and fresh vegetables.

Each serving provides 298 kcal, 12g protein, 52g carbohydrates (of which 16g sugars), 1.6g fat (of which 10g saturates), 10g fibre and 0.4g salt.

Servings: 4   Cooking Time: 30 Mins.-1 Hour

Ingredients:

- 3 celery sticks, roughly chopped
- 2 carrots, peeled and roughly chopped
- 1 large sweet potato, scrubbed and cut into 3cm/1¼in chunks
- 1 onion, chopped
- 2 garlic cloves, crushed
- 6 thyme sprigs, leaves only, or 1 tsp dried thyme
- 400g tin chopped tomatoes
- 1 tsp ground turmeric
- 1 tsp ground allspice
- ½ tsp chilli powder
- 2 x 400g tins black-eyed beans, drained and rinsed
- 1 lime, juice only
- salt and freshly ground black pepper
- To serve
- 6 spring onions, shredded
- lime wedges

Directions:

1. Combine all of the ingredients, except the black-eye beans and lime juice, in a large saucepan or casserole. Pour in 600ml/20fl oz water, bring to the boil, then reduce the heat. Cover and simmer gently for 25 minutes until the vegetables are soft but still holding their shape.
2. Stir in the beans, bring back to a simmer and cook uncovered for 10 minutes, stirring occasionally. Remove from the heat, stir in the lime juice and season with salt and plenty of black pepper. Spoon the stew into bowls, top with the shredded spring onions and serve with lime wedges.

Pumpkin Stew With Sour Cream

This lentil and pumpkin stew is all about how to make a straightforward recipe a lot more exciting - with very little effort. Perfect for when it's cooling down outside and you want something really warming.
Each serving provides 273kcal, 8g protein, 28g carbohydrate (of which 14g sugars), 12g fat (of which 7g saturates), 9g fibre and 2g salt.

Servings: 4   **Cooking Time: 30 Mins.-1 Hour**

Ingredients:

- 40g/1½oz butter
- 2 onions, chopped
- 1 carrot, chopped
- 1 stick celery, chopped
- 3 sprigs rosemary
- 2 bay leaves
- 1 clove garlic, chopped
- 400g/14oz lentils
- 1.2litres/2pints 2fl oz vegetable stock
- 600g/1lb 5oz assorted pumpkin or squash (total chopped weight)
- small bunch parsley, chopped
- 2 tbsp red wine vinegar
- 4 tbsp sour cream

Directions:

1. In a large pan melt the butter and then add chopped onions, carrot and celery. Tear in the rosemary and a couple of bay leaves and after a few minutes add the chopped garlic. When all have nicely softened, tip in the lentils and pour over 1litre/1¾ pints of vegetable stock. Bring to the boil and then leave to simmer whilst you tend to the pumpkin.
2. Using a variety of pumpkins and squashes gives the stew a more complex flavour. Here I use acorn squash and Cinderella, but you want to end up with about 600g/1lb 5oz of peeled pumpkin in large chunks. Add them to the stew, season and then pour over enough water to just cover all the ingredients. Put a lid on the pan and leave to simmer for 30-40 minutes.
3. When the stew is almost ready, add the chopped parsley.
4. To make the stew creamier, remove a small bowlful to a food processor and blitz it with 200ml/2fl oz of stock. Pour it back in and the stew becomes instantly more velvety.
5. Serve the stew in bowls, finishing each helping off with a cooling spoonful of sour cream.

Pulled Jackfruit Coconut Stew

Jackfruit is a fantastic meat replacement. It absorbs flavours wonderfully and, in this coconut stew, takes on a variety of wonderful spicy flavours. Serve with freshly cooked rice.

Each serving (without the rice) provides 192 kcal, 4g protein, 13.5g carbohydrates (of which 10g sugars), 12g fat (of which 8g saturates), 7.5g fibre and 1.4g salt.

Servings: 4   Cooking Time: 30 Mins.-1 Hour

Ingredients:

- 520g/1lb 3oz green jackfruit, rinsed and drained
- 1 tsp sea salt flakes
- 1 tsp freshly ground black pepper
- 1 tsp paprika
- 1 tsp dried thyme
- 1 tsp allspice
- 1 tbsp olive oil
- 1 brown onion, chopped
- 2 garlic cloves, minced
- 400g tin chopped tomatoes
- 200ml/7fl oz coconut milk
- ½ Scotch bonnet or other chilli
- 1 red pepper, seeds removed, sliced
- 1 green pepper, seeds removed, sliced
- 150ml/5fl oz vegetable stock or water

Directions:

1. Bring a saucepan of water to the boil, add the jackfruit and cook until tender (about 10 minutes). Drain well and pull into shreds using a fork. Season with the salt, black pepper, paprika, thyme and allspice and mix together. Set aside.
2. Meanwhile, heat the oil in a frying pan over a medium heat. Add the onion and garlic and cook for 3 minutes, until softened. Add the tomatoes and coconut milk and mix together, then add the whole chilli and cook for 15–20 minutes. Add the peppers, vegetable stock and jackfruit and cook until the sauce is reduced and the peppers are cooked. Take out the chilli before serving.
3. Serve in warmed bowls with the rice.

Notes:

1. If serving this to a vegan, check that the vegetable stock is suitable for vegans.

Chickpea Stew With Tomatoes And Green Chilli

This hearty vegetarian stew is quick and easy to prepare. Serve with yoghurt and pitta breads. Each serving provides 257kcal, 11g protein, 27g carbohydrate (of which 7g sugars), 10g fat (of which 1g saturates), 10g fibre and 1.3g salt.

Servings: 4   Cooking Time: 10-30 Mins.

Ingredients:

- 2 tbsp olive oil
- 1 red onion, finely sliced
- 3 garlic cloves, finely sliced
- 2 teaspoons freshly grated ginger
- 1 or 2 green chillies, to taste, seeded and finely chopped
- 1 tsp sea salt
- 2 X 400g/14oz tins of chickpeas, drained
- 80ml/2¾fl oz water
- 1 tsp cumin
- 1 tsp turmeric, optional
- freshly ground black pepper
- 500g/17½oz cherry tomatoes
- 100g/3½oz baby English spinach leaves
- To serve
- plain yoghurt
- pitta bread
- olive oil
- salt and freshly ground black pepper
- paprika

Directions:

1. Heat a large deep frying pan over a medium to high heat.
2. Add the oil, onion, garlic, ginger, chillies and salt and cook for five minutes (or until the onions are soft) being careful to stir regularly.
3. Add the chickpeas, 80ml/2¾fl oz water, cumin, turmeric and pepper and cook for five minutes or until the water evaporates.
4. Add the tomatoes and cook for another two minutes to soften.
5. Remove from the heat and check for seasoning.
6. Stir through the spinach and top with yoghurt.
7. To make the pitta crisps, break up pieces of pitta bread and drizzle with olive oil, salt, pepper and paprika.
8. Bake in a moderate oven for 10-12 minutes or until crisp.
9. Serve with the stew on a warmed plate.

Peanut Stew

This luxurious peanut stew combines chickpeas, spinach, peanut butter and spices to make a warming, comforting vegan dish. Great served with freshly cooked rice, lime wedges, chopped coriander and red chilli.
Each serving provides 301 kcal, 10g protein, 36g carbohydrates (of which 10g sugars), 11g fat (of which 2g saturates), 10g fibre and 0.3g salt.

Servings: 4 **Cooking Time: 30 Mins.-1 Hour**

Ingredients:

- For the peanut stew
- 1 tbsp olive oil
- 1 brown onion, finely chopped
- 1 red pepper, seeds removed and roughly chopped
- 2 large garlic cloves, grated
- ½cm/1/5 in piece ginger, peeled and grated
- 1 tbsp ground coriander
- ½ tbsp ground cumin
- 3 heaped tbsp smooth peanut butter
- 500ml/18fl oz vegetable stock
- 2 medium sweet potatoes, peeled and cut into bite-size pieces
- 1 x 400g/14oz tin chickpeas, drained
- 80g/3oz spinach
- salt and freshly ground black pepper

Directions:

1. Heat the olive oil in a large saucepan over a medium heat, then add the onion and pepper, stirring regularly until softened, about 5 minutes.
2. Add the garlic, ginger and spices and stir continuously until aromatic, about 20 seconds.
3. Add the peanut butter and stock, then add the sweet potato and chickpeas. Cook with the lid on for about 25 minutes or until the sweet potato is cooked through.
4. Add the spinach for the last 2 minutes, so it wilts but doesn't overcook. Season with salt and pepper and serve.

Flexible Lentil Stew

Easy and affordable, this simple recipe for lentil stew is ideal for batch cooking and can be used in different ways throughout the week.

Servings: 6   **Cooking Time: 30 Mins.-1 Hour**

Ingredients:

- For the basic lentil stew
- 1 tbsp oil, for frying
- 1 large onion, finely chopped
- 2 celery sticks, finely chopped
- 2 medium carrots, finely chopped
- 2 large garlic cloves, crushed
- 400g/14oz potatoes, peeled and cut into 1–2cm/½–¾in cubes
- 2 fresh thyme sprigs, leaves picked
- 2 fresh rosemary sprigs, leaves finely chopped
- 250g/9oz dried green lentils, washed
- 1 litre/1¾ pints hot vegetable stock
- 15g/½oz fresh parsley, finely chopped
- 1 tbsp white wine or cider vinegar
- For the butternut squash and spinach curried lentils
- 1 tbsp coconut oil
- 1 red onion, roughly chopped
- 350g/12oz butternut squash, cut into 2cm/¾in cubes
- 1 tbsp curry powder
- 3 tbsp Thai red curry paste
- 400ml tin coconut milk
- ½ tbsp runny honey
- 500g/1lb 2oz lentil stew
- 150g/5½oz baby spinach leaves
- jasmine rice, to serve
- fresh coriander, to serve
- dairy or coconut yoghurt, to serve
- sea salt and cracked black pepper

Directions:

1. To make the basic lentil stew, heat the oil in a large frying pan over a medium heat. Add the onion, celery and carrot and gently fry for 5–6 minutes until they begin to soften. Add the garlic along with a generous pinch of salt and fry for a further 1–2 minutes.
2. Add the cubed potato to the pan along with the thyme and rosemary. Tip in the washed lentils and stir through the vegetables. Pour in the stock and bring to the boil.
3. Turn down the heat to medium-low and simmer for 30–35 minutes until the lentils are cooked but still holding shape. Stir frequently to ensure it doesn't stick to the pan. If the stock is reducing too rapidly, add a lid and lower the heat.
4. When the lentils are cooked al dente, remove the pan from the heat and sprinkle in the parsley and vinegar. Stir well and season to taste with salt and pepper.
5. At this stage, your lentil stew can be portioned up and frozen in bags or tubs for a quick homemade meal to eat another day. You can serve it straight away, or bring it back to life as butternut squash and spinach curried lentils.
6. To make the butternut squash and spinach curried lentils, heat the coconut oil in a frying pan over a medium-high heat. Add the onion and fry for 4–5 minutes until it begins to soften. Add the butternut squash and curry powder and stir.
7. Spoon in the curry paste and stir to coat the squash. Pour in the coconut milk plus half a tin of water. Stir through the honey and gently simmer for 10 minutes.
8. Add the 2 portions of lentil stew to the pan and continue to simmer for another 10–15 minutes. Remove from the heat, season if required with salt and pepper, then stir through the spinach to wilt. Serve with the jasmine rice, topped with a few fresh coriander leaves and dollop of yoghurt.

Versatile Vegetable Stew

You can add any veg you like to this versatile stew. Just add root vegetables and squash at the beginning, green vegetables towards the end and frozen peas or sweetcorn at the last minute. Adding baked beans adds a little sweetness, plus fibre and protein.

Each serving provides 162 kcal, 7g protein, 25g carbohydrates (of which 10g sugars), 2.5g fat (of which 0.5g saturates), 8g fibre and 0.4g salt.

Servings: 8   Cooking Time: 10-30 Mins.

Ingredients:

- 1 tbsp olive oil
- 1 onion, finely diced
- 2 leeks, split lengthways up to the root several times, washed under running cold water then sliced thickly
- 2 carrots, cut into 1cm/½in dice
- 2 garlic cloves, finely diced
- 1 tsp sweet smoked paprika
- ½ tsp dried thyme
- 2 potatoes, peeled, cut into 1cm/½in dice
- 600ml/21fl oz vegetable stock
- ½ head cauliflower, cut into small florets
- 200g/7oz fine green beans, cut into 2cm/¾in pieces
- 1 x 400g/14oz tin baked beans
- 2 tbsp roughly chopped flatleaf parsley
- crusty bread, to serve
- salt and freshly ground black pepper

Directions:

1. Heat a large frying pan or saucepan until medium hot, add the olive oil, onion and leeks and cook gently for 5 minutes until just softened.
2. Add the carrots, garlic, paprika and thyme and stir to combine. Cook for 5 minutes.
3. Add the potatoes and vegetable stock and bring to the boil. Turn the heat down and simmer for 5 minutes until the potatoes are just softening then add the cauliflower and simmer for another 5 minutes.
4. By now, all the vegetables should be nearly cooked. Add the green beans and baked beans and cook for 3 minutes then stir in the chopped parsley and season well with salt and pepper.
5. Serve with plenty of crusty bread.

Easy Mexican Bean Stew

Try this easy Mexican bean stew that's mostly made from store cupboard ingredients. It's surprisingly healthy and makes a quick and filling midweek dinner.

Servings: 2 **Cooking Time: 30 Mins.-1 Hour**

Ingredients:

- low-calorie cooking spray
- 1 onion, thinly sliced
- 2 garlic cloves, crushed
- 1 yellow pepper, deseeded and cut into 3cm/1in chunks
- ½ tsp hot chilli powder
- 1 tsp ground cumin
- 1 tsp ground coriander
- 400g tin chopped tomatoes
- 2 tbsp tomato purée
- 400g tin mixed beans, drained and rinsed
- 125g/4½oz brown rice, to serve
- 100g/3½oz fat-free Greek yoghurt, to serve
- 1 lime, cut into wedges, to serve
- salt and freshly ground black pepper
- For the salsa
- 1 tomato, roughly chopped
- 4 tbsp roughly chopped freshly coriander
- 2 spring onions, thinly sliced

Directions:

1. Spray a large frying pan with oil and place over a medium heat. Add the onion and garlic and cook gently for three minutes, stirring regularly. Add the pepper and cook for two minutes.
2. Stir in the spices and cook for a few seconds, then add the tomatoes, tomato purée and mixed beans. Pour over 300ml/10fl oz cold water and bring to a gentle simmer. Season with a little salt and lots of ground black pepper and cook for 30 minutes, stirring occasionally until thick.
3. Meanwhile half-fill a medium saucepan with water and bring to the boil. Add the rice and return to the boil. Cook for 25 minutes, or until tender, stirring occasionally.
4. To make the salsa, mix the tomato, coriander and spring onions together in a bowl.
5. Drain the rice and divide between two plates. Spoon the beans over and scatter with the salsa. Serve with the yoghurt and lime wedges.

Cannellini Bean And Pea Stew

Servings: 4 **Cooking Time: 10-30 Mins.**

Ingredients:

- 2 tbsp olive oil, plus extra to garnish
- 200g/7oz red onion, finely diced
- 200g/7oz celery, finely diced and leaves reserved for garnish
- 200g/7oz red pepper, finely diced
- 3 garlic cloves, grated
- 2 tsp paprika
- 2 tsp dried mixed herbs
- 1 vegetable stock cube
- 1 tbsp cornflour or plain flour
- 400g tin cannellini beans, drained and rinsed
- 2 tbsp tomato purée
- 300g/10½oz frozen peas
- salt and freshly ground black pepper

Directions:

1. Heat the oil in a large saucepan or casserole over a medium heat and add the onion, celery and red pepper. Season well with salt and pepper and fry for around 7–8 minutes or until softened. Add the garlic, paprika and herbs and stir for another 2 minutes.
2. Measure out 600ml/20fl oz hot water in a jug and crumble in the stock cube. Add the cornflour and stir to combine. Pour into the pan along with the beans and tomato purée. Bring to a gentle simmer for 5 minutes. Add the peas and simmer over a low heat for another 5 minutes.
3. Serve the stew in warmed bowls and garnish with a little of the reserved celery leaf, a drizzle of olive oil and a sprinkle of black pepper.

Printed in Great Britain
by Amazon